Teaching Swimming: Fun and Effective Instruction

Jeffrey Napolski

Swim Instructor Training Workbook

Swimming Ideas, LLC
https://swimminglessonsideas.com

3rd Edition, 2019

Teaching Swimming: Fun and Effective Instruction, Swim Instructor Training Workbook

Copyright © 2019 www.swimminglessonsideas.com Swimming Ideas, LLC

Contributing Author: Jeffrey Napolski

All rights reserved. Items may be reproduced by purchasers for personal or company educational use. No part of the book may be reproduced, sold or distributed in any form without written permission of the publisher.

Published by Swimming Ideas, LLC

500 Park Ave.

Libertyville, IL 60048

Printed in USA

Contents

Going Underwater— 4
Free motion and play— 6
Supported Front Glides— 8
Supported Back Glides— 12
Worksheet and Discussion #1— 16
Flutter Kick— 18
Streamline— 20
Front Crawl Arms - Freestyle— 22
Freestyle Breathing— 26
Backstroke Arms— 32
Breaststroke Kick— 36
Breaststroke Arms— 38
Butterfly Kick— 42
Butterfly Arms— 44
Flip turns— 46
Open Turns— 48
How to teach: Method and Delivery— 52
Using Command Language— 54
Remove "okay" from your sentences— 56
Earning Trust— 58
Using Images— 60
Constant Feedback— 62
Praise and Feedback Types— 64
Feedback Layer Cake— 68
Total Active Engagement— 70
One on One— 72
Rotation Method— 74
Waves— 76
Maximizing Action— 78
Time on Task— 80
Lesson Plan Organization— 82
Progressions and Flow— 84
How to handle going underwater— 86
Incremental Underwater Progression— 88
Addressing Fear— 90
Dunking versus Scooping— 94
Scooping progression— 96
Parent and Infant: How to hold— 98
Worksheet 1 answers— 102
Worksheet 2 answers— 103
Worksheet 3 answers— 104
Worksheet 4 answers— 105
Thank you! Good luck!— 106

Going Underwater

First step to learning how to swim.

Go slow. Build trust with gradual incremental progression.

Ask repeatedly if swimmer will go under.

Once you master going underwater it may seem like a super simple and easy thing to do. For children who haven't experienced what it feels like to be underwater comfortably it is a terrifying prospect.

We want to make going underwater for our participants fun and exciting, interesting and amusing.

Swimming Ideas recommends that you take a gradual and slow approach to encouraging children to go underwater at their own pace.

Provide multiple opportunities to go underwater through games, activities, challenges, and asking questions to get kids to put their face underwater.

With continued effort, with constant asking and offering opportunities the swimmers will eventually join in the fun and put their faces underwater to begin their swimming journey.

What was it like for you the first time you went underwater? Do you remember it?

Do you have a personal story about your first moments in a swimming pool. Take some time to think about how you learned to swim or how you got comfortable being in and around the water.

How can you ensure that your swimmers will have a joyful and safe learning moment?

When working with a swimmer who does not go underwater follow the steps of the "underwater progression."

Underwater Progression:
1. Chest
2. Shoulders
3. Chin
4. Lips
5. Nose
6. Eyes
7. Whole head

Build Trust over time

- Earn trust. Be honest.
- Demonstrate first.
- Respect swimmer choices

Ask often.

- "Do you want to go under?"
- Kiss the water, put your nose in. How about your chin?

Incremental steps

- Go slowly. Start with 1 build up to 7.
- Avoid jumping steps.

Underwater Progression

Go slow. Ask swimmers to go underwater to their level of comfort. If your swimmer is apprehensive, scared, or reluctant, ask them to first put their shoulders in the water.

If they do that, then begin asking them to do the next step of the progression. If a swimmer puts their chin in the water, ask them to "kiss the water" so their lips go in.

Avoid jumping steps of this progression.

You will get push back, and reluctance.

"Do you want to go under?"

Jumps are an excellent way to build trust with your swimmers.

Jumps can be scary, they can be fun, and they can be a wonderful tool in your skill bank to demonstrate to your swimmers that they can trust you.

Every time you do a jump from the side, even with reluctant swimmers, ask, "Do you want to go underwater?"

If they say no, help them jump in keeping their face above water. Over time they'll start saying "yes!"

Games - Bake a Cake

Play games designed to get your beginner swimmers to willingly put their faces in the water. Fill your lessons with games.

Games distract swimmers from their fear and if we join in their imaginary worlds we can encourage high levels of participation from our swimmers.

Get into the make-believe world with your participants. Fill the silence with narrative, "What do you want to put in the cake? Bananas? I love bananas. Help me chop them up and splash them in?"

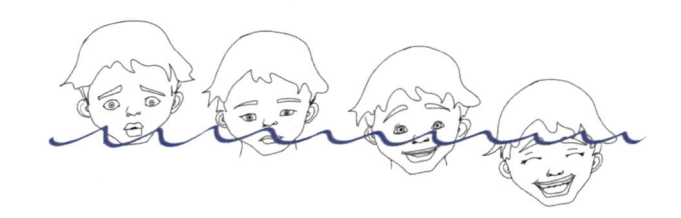

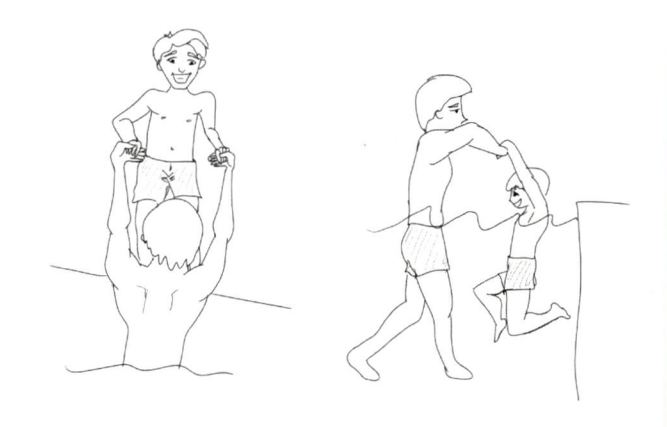

Free motion and play

Learn to move independently.

Supervise closely, even with a life-jacket. Younger swimmers may not be able to lift their heads out of water.

Use life-jackets to learn movement.

Get a life jacket and secure straps around body. You'll want to have a soft full wrapped life jacket instead of the old generic old around the neck only life jackets.

Safety Item:

Closely monitor any swimmers in life jackets until they learn how to turn themselves over from front to back under their own power. We don't want to have our swimmers drop their heads in the water and be unable to lift them up on their own. If a swimmer gets stuck on their front or back, they won't be able to recover and save themselves unless they know how to push the water with their hands and rotate around their center of buoyancy.

Life Jacket motion:

Take time to move around in water you can stand in while wearing a life jacket. You have two main goals to attain here:

- Discover how to recover from a face down position and rotate either to the back, or lift the head up out of the water.

- Discover how pushing the water with your hand makes your body move and learn how to propel body forward, backward, and around using kicks and arm motions of any kind.

Engage in any type of game, movement, or action in your life jacket. Play catch, fetch with a ball or toy, play tag, any game you can think of to become familiar with moving through the water. Movement and motion are primary.

Move around

- Set targets. Go to them.
- Encourage swimmers to paddle with arms and kick.
- Use hands to rotate body and move self forward.

Play games

- Dump toys in water and have swimmer collect them while wearing jacket.
- Race to a set location.
- Challenges to spin body.

Independence

- Let swimmers move alone.
- Avoid helping too much.

Independent Motion

Encourage swimmers to use their arms and hands as paddles to move themselves around the pool and water.

Play games like races, obstacle courses, or physical challenges to build comfort and provide motion.

Can the swimmer go from belly down to belly up while wearing a jacket? Help them out and have them practice in shallow water.

Walk around the shallow end in life-jackets first, then move to deeper water as swimmers get comfortable.

Find the right fit

Make sure your swimmers wear the appropriate size life-jacket.

If you put a jacket on a swimmer that is too big, it may fall off, the swimmer might fall out, or it could possibly restrict breathing. A wrong size life-jacket is ineffective and should be avoided.

Make sure that you have a variety of life-jacket sizes to provide to your swimmers.

Too small, and it might not support the swimmer's weight. Too big, and it might fall off.

Play games and get comfy

Spend time in the life-jackets and even do the glides and floats with the jackets on.

They can provide a great sense of safety and comfort for beginning swimmers.

Take advantage of lowered anxiety and encourage swimmers to use their hands and feet to move themselves around the water.

Play different games and go to different areas of the pool all while wearing the life jackets.

Supported Front Glides

Build confidence in floating.

Relax with body flat at surface.

Encourage putting the face in the water.

The Script:

- "Put your shoulders in the water"
- "Reach our arms out in front of you."
- "Put your [chin, lips, nose, eyes, face] in the water."
- "Push off with me."

Repeat this script over and over every time you initiate a front glide with your swimmers.

Telling swimmers to "put their shoulders" in the water gives them a command, or a target for them to accomplish. It is language designed to get a reaction instead of detailing out exactly what the swimmer should do in too much excruciating detail.

Remember to be supportive. Build trust by going slow. There is no need to rush through this progression of supported front glides.

Take your time. Begin close to the swimmer. Let them know, feel, and understand that they can put their safety and their lives in your hands and that you will not let them go.

Keep your swimmer's face above water if they do not like going under. Avoid letting them sink or be unsupported in any way.

To beginners, removing support while away from where they can stand or over a bench is like dropping them from a height. They will sink under immediately and panic.

Build trust. Earn their comfort by going slow and establishing habits and feel for the water by holding them at or near the surface using the "hands on shoulders," or "hands in instructor's hands" methods.

Build trust

- Prove to swimmer they can trust you by always holding them up.
- Say the same things, follow the same steps; repetition builds trust.

Begin close

- Let swimmer reach for your shoulders before you push off with them.
- As comfort grows, have them reach farther to get to your shoulders.

Shoulders in!

- Put your shoulders in the water too. Get at eye level with the swimmers.

Hands on shoulders

Participant places their hands on the instructor's shoulders.

Keep swimmer's arms straight and attempt to keep body straight. This support is usually used for swimmers that do not put their face in the water. Lift the belly or outside of hips to manipulate the swimmer's body into a straight line.

If possible, encourage swimmer to put their face in the water. Instructor should walk backwards to simulate movement and independent propulsion.

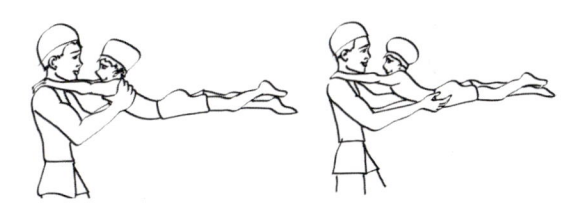

Hands in Instructor's hand

Participant reaches forward in streamline with their face in the water.

The instructor will hold the participant's hands with their own. Push hands to surface and pull to provide motion.

Hold the swimmer at arms length, if needed, use other hand to support belly and body.

Goal is to keep participant's arms straight.

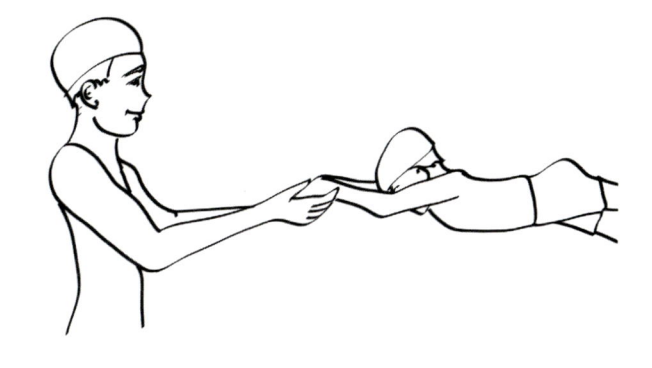

Short glide, then supported.

Instructor stands a body length or two away from participant and waits for swimmer to glide to them.

Goal is for participant to glide with their face down, in the water keeping their body straight.

Once participant gets to instructor, either support with hands on shoulders or hands supported on instructor's hand.

Can also provide support with fingertips under swimmer's palms.

Supported Front Glides continued:

- Keep body straight as possible.

- Build trust through constant support.

We start doing supported front glides with the exact same hand holds with infants.

This is a crucial skill and activity for all beginner swimmers.

Your main challenge will be to keep your shoulders in the water and near the water line without allowing your swimmer to slip underwater or get too egregiously splashed in the face.

Yes, we want to encourage putting the face in the water, but we do not want to rush the process.

Put significant effort into encouraging a straight flat body that is relaxed.

We want the swimmer to place their weight in their hands on your shoulders and relax the rest of their body to "float" on the surface.

Force their hips up by walking backwards. The flow of water under the swimmer's body will lift them to the surface.

Put your face in the water while talking and encouraging swimmer to do the same.

Tell swimmers to kick with small and large splashes. You can make a game out of splashing parts of the pool near your area or other people (within reason).

Kicking will help get the body near the surface.

Kicking will be the first mode of propulsion for many new swimmers.

- Keep the swimmer near or at the surface.

- Allow face to remain out of water, but encourage swimmer to put it in. Begin with "kissing the water."

- Walk backwards to "float" or lift swimmer's body.

Other ways to practice:

Lay flat in shallow

Alligator walks

Zero depth pool

Use props like kick-boards

Change things up by allowing your swimmers to use kick-boards, barbells, or other float devices instead of you.

Let them cross short distances with the aid of a floating tool.

Keep a hand on the kickboard to increase confidence.

Encourage a strong kick to make the participant move on their own.

Swimmers can choose to put their face in or not.

Put your shoulders under!

You can see from the picture to the right that the swimmer isn't putting their arms in front of them.

Look at the raised head. Yes, it is in the water, but we want the face aimed at the bottom of the pool. You can see the swimmer is clutching the instructor's forearms.

This is NOT an effective way to hold for supported front glides.

Instructor should get their shoulders IN the water. Swimmer should put his hands on top of her shoulders and put face in water looking directly down.

Why float? Glide!

Skip the floats. Go straight into gliding.

Why? If you can glide, you can float. I think floating is fun, entertaining, and exciting. It makes for a great challenge.

If we're maximizing our teaching time, and remember our goal is fun and effective swim lessons, then we can skip teaching floats. Spend your valuable time and effort on teaching glides and floats will come naturally as a result of your instruction. We want forward horizontal motion.

Supported Back Glides

Swimmers are upsidedown, backwards, and vulnerable. Be supportive!

Start low to avoid face slipping under.

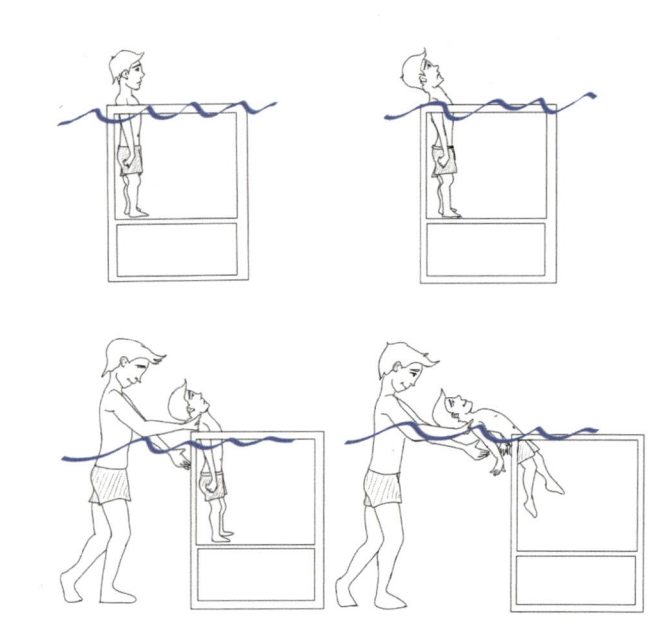

The Script:
- "Turn away from me."
- "Put your shoulders in the water."
- "Tilt your head back."
- "Push off with me."

There are three levels of support for back glides.

1) Swimmer's head resting on your shoulder with a cheek to cheek connection.

2) Swimmer's head resting in your palm with your other hand supporting their lower back.

3) Swimmer's neck supported by your two fingertips.

Going slow and at the swimmer's comfort is extremely important for this skill. People who cannot float on their own, or move in the water, or are afraid of going underwater will be afraid of doing back glides.

Earn their trust by demonstrating one of the holds with another willing child first.

Get close. Get their head on your shoulder and press your cheek into their face. The cheek to cheek connection will soothe most hesitant swimmers, especially infants.

This is generally appropriate up to about age 5; older move directly to the hand under the swimmer's head position.

Open your hand. Put your palm up. Notice how your thumb and pointer finger create a cradle, or a web. Push that web between your thumb and pointer finger into the back of the child's neck so that the child's skull rests on your palm.

If using your right hand, then your thumb would be pointed to the right and fingers wrapped around the child's neck. Let the back of the head rest in your palm.

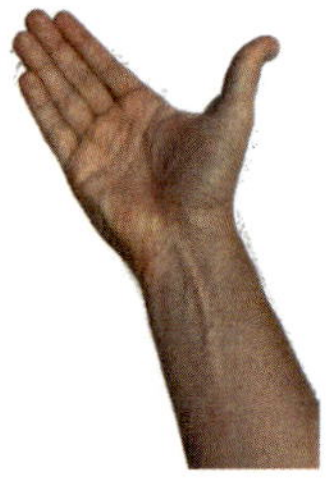

Head on shoulder

Head in hand

Fingers on neck

12

Provide Comfort

Keep contact with the swimmer when doing the Head in Hand hold. Notice in picture to right how the instructor is touching the swimmer's forehead.

This accomplishes two things: 1) Comforts the swimmer to reassure that the instructor is still there helping. 2) Tilts head back to make sure ears remain in the water.

Most beginners will crane their neck to their chest to avoid putting their ears in the water.

They fear not seeing and being backwards.

Arms in soldier

Avoid doing back glides with the arms out in airplane. Instead, do glides with the body in soldier, as seen in the black line drawing to the right.

In the color picture, the swimmer's arms are in airplane. Avoid doing this on back glides.

Encourage swimmers to scull near their hips, or make small motions to keep their tummies at the surface or to touch their bellies or hold a toy.

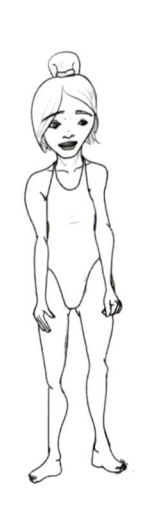

Soldier Glides First

Young swimmers will find streamline on their back difficult. Reserve Back Streamlines for swimmers comfortable doing back glides in soldier.

Have your level 1 and level 2 swimmers focus primarily on back glides in soldier. It is easier to tilt the head back and get the belly up when the arms are near the hips.

Encourage swimmers to scull, or make small motions near hips to keep body at surface. We can also hold the head better with arms at sides.

Supported Back Glides continued:

Avoid curving body

Correct wrong holding immediately! Teach good habits instead.

We always want the swimmer's feet pushing perpendicular to our chest, or their feet aiming in the same direction as our belly buttons.

Not the picture at the top right with two examples. The left picture has the feet aiming at our point of view. That is correct. Notice how the swimmer's feet and the instructor's belly butt is pointing in the same direction.

Look at the picture next to it. The swimmer looks like they are a wet noodle, or a sack of sand melting through the instructor's hands.

Do not hold the swimmer sideways, or with your arms under their back and legs.

Doing this will create a "banana" shape to the swimmer's body and when they go to do a glide on their own they will sink to the bottom or struggle.

Our goal is to get swimmers who are terrified of being on their back or unable to glide on their back to comfortably move across the water while staying afloat at the surface on their backs.

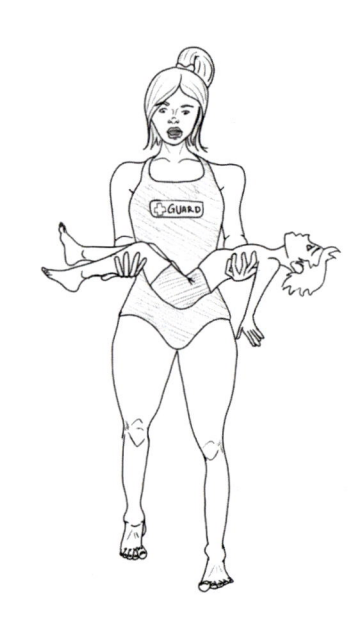

When teaching supported back glides support the head and neck with minimal yet supportive touches and holds.
If we hold the head and the neck then the swimmer is responsible for lifting their body. When they transition to doing glides on their own they will have already established their body position as a habit and will easier transition to unsupported back glides.

Lower your shoulders in the water and remain as close to swimmer's head as possible. Maintain a constant stream of words or sing songs like "Twinkle Twinkle" to distract swimmers and remind them that you are there and helping. Earn trust, go slow, support their heads.

Support the head
- Hold the neck or the back of the head, using free hand to adjust forehead tilt or lift belly.
- Keep face above water.

"Push your belly up"
- Tell swimmers to adjust their body on their own.
- "Let your belly button breathe"
- "Make splashes!"

Body line
- Move through water to get body to straighten out. Moving water will help lift feet to the surface.

Wrong holding #1:

Instructor has their hands under the lower back and the knees. Look how the swimmer is not submerged at all, and has no control over their body.

See the outstretched arms of the swimmer? This is to balance the awkward placement of the instructor's hands.

Look at the raised head. We want swimmer's ears in the water with a neutral float where face remains above and ears in.

What would happen if the instructor let go?

Wrong holding #2:

That swimmer does not look happy. Look at that grimace!

Instructor is holding the waist while the swimmer throws their arms to the side and lifts their head like they are about to fall onto pavement.

Swimmer's entire head is lifted above the water and weight is pressed into the instructor's hands.

What would happen to the swimmer if the instructor let go?

Does the second swimmer look happy?

Wrong holding #3:

This is what happens when we have swimmers that aren't ready for streamline do it on their back.

The arms are not in correct streamline position.

Face is completely submerged, which for many beginners is both terrifying and uncomfortable (why?).

If instructor was behind the swimmer's head pulling on the hands locked together it might be better. Avoid streamline until the swimmer is comfortable with underwater swimming.

Worksheet and Discussion #1

1) What is the underwater progression?

2) What does incremental progression mean?

3) If we ask a swimmer, "Do you want to go underwater" and they say, "no," should you pull them underwater? Why?

4) What is the supported front glide script?

5) When working with young swimmers in shallow water why is it important for the instructor to put their shoulders in the water too?

6) What are the benefits of demonstrating a swim skill first? Who can do the demonstrations?

7) Is it better to lead through fear or respect and trust?

Discussion topic #1: Fear

Notes:

Going underwater and doing supported front glides and back glides can be terrifying.

What are some elements of swim lessons that might be scary for a new participant?

Do those fears change or become more expressed based on the age of the swimmer?

What are infants afraid of?

What about toddlers (2-4 years old)?

What are 5+ afraid of?

Discussion topic #2: Underwater

Notes:

Should we dunk our swimmers?

Have you heard the phrase "sink or swim?" Do you have an experience with being tossed in the water and forced to either survive or sink to the bottom of the water?

Does throwing someone that doesn't know how to swim provide a benefit?

What are the positives of gentle, loving, gradual encouragement over throwing someone in without help?

Discussion topic #3: Floats

Notes:

Should you do floats before glides?

We skipped floats deliberately. Why?

What are the benefits of teaching stationary floating?

Can you achieve the same goals with skipping straight to glides?

Is there any value to teaching horizontal forward progress or motion over stationary floating?

Flutter Kick

Used for Freestyle and Backstroke

Begins at the hip and flows down through the toes.

Ankles should be "floppy"

Flutter kicking is the kick that most people think of when swimming.

The legs move in parallel, alternating one up and the other down.

Initiate the kick by flexing the hips and glutes, snapping the knees, and pushing the water with the top and bottom of your foot.

For beginners encourage them to make splashes with their feet.

Hold their thighs just above the knee and move up and down. Can also grasp shins just below the knee to similar effect.

Encourage splashing initially, then transition to underwater kicks that "boil" the water.

For advanced swimmers flutter kick is two alternating butterfly kicks where the hip begins the undulation and rolls through the knee and ankle.

When doing supported front and back glides have swimmers make splashes, or do their flutter kicks.

When you are having swimmers move back and forth from bench to bench or crossing short distances have them do flutter kicks to provide propulsion.

Most beginners will use their legs to make themselves move forward first, and understand how to push the water with their hands after.

Focus on a good kick that makes them move forward.

Play games and do activities that look for a result: make a splash hit the lifeguard using only your feet, fill this bucket with water only using your legs, send this floating toy into the ocean by making splashes with your feet while sitting on the side.

Start big, tighten with skill.

Floppy ankles

- Foot should be limp, floppy or moveable.
- Knee bends a little. Too much bending not good.
- Toes move like paint brush; flowing up / down.

Boil the water

- Ultimate goal is underwater kicks that boil the surface with their force.
- Avoid excessive splashes as mastery increases.
- Beginners can splash!

Constant kick

- Teach kicking habit early.
- Keep kick going even when breathing.

Kicking on the side

Begin teaching flutter kick while sitting on the edge of the pool. Extend legs straight into the water and make splashes.

Avoid very bendy knees and instead promote a slight bend while feet flop in the water.

Push water up and down with the top and bottom of the foot.

Kick originates with the hips. If possible get butt to lean on the edge of the deck so that most of the leg goes in the water.

Kick with support

Physically manipulate the legs by kicking for the beginner swimmer. Grasp above or below the knees and move in small quick up and down motions.

Have swimmer hold the wall and if possible put face in the water. Alternately, have them hold the back or rail of a bench.

Encourage kicking while doing supported front glides and back glides. Can move feet for them while they hold your shoulder or rest in your support.

Goal here is to kick enough to get body at surface.

Kicks to move

We recommend you do a LOT of glides using flutter kicks to move from one bench to another.

Push the benches closer together to begin with and use kicks to cross the distance. Give assistance devices like barbells, kick-boards, or life-jackets at first.

When comfort grows have swimmers cross the widening distance of the benches with their face in the water and aiming down. Swimmers should kick with arms outstretched in position 11 to cross the gap.

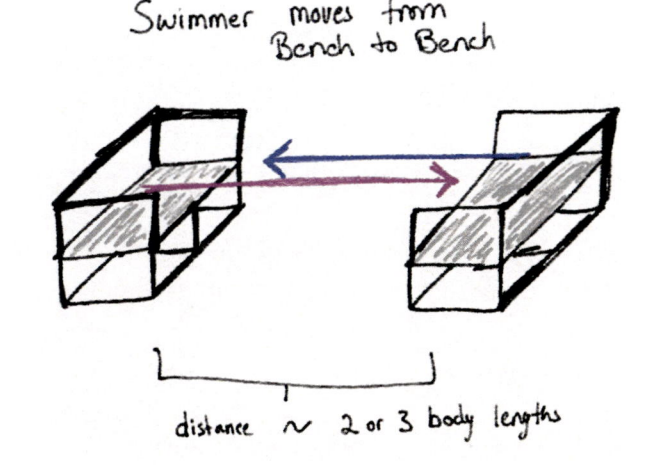

Streamline

Enforce all three facets of good streamlines.

Begin everything with a streamline.

Fastest and easiest part of swimming.

The Script:

- Lock your thumb.
- Squeeze your ears.
- Look down.

Repeat these three crucial parts to streamline and enforce compliance with them and you'll have your swimmers performing this critical element of all swimming.

Begin by demonstrating while standing on the deck or where swimmers can stand comfortably.

Place one hand on top of the other and wrap the top hand's thumb around the pink part of the palm on the hand under.

Lock it in.

Squeeze the elbows around the head, near the back over the ears. Avoid squeezing the eyes.

Aim face in the same direction as the belly button. Avoid curving back, bending elbows, and a tucked chin.

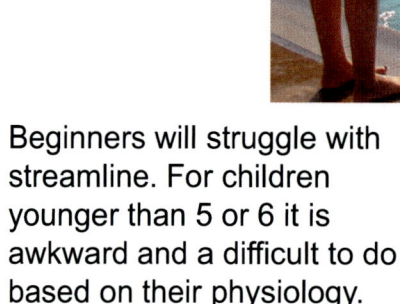

Beginners will struggle with streamline. For children younger than 5 or 6 it is awkward and a difficult to do based on their physiology.

Swimmers will feel unbalanced and want to lift their heads up to "see" where they are going.

Repeat like a continual mantra "aim your face down," look down, or drag your Pinocchio nose along the bottom of the pool.

Advanced swimmers should do streamline before every single activity. If they push off the wall it should be in streamline.

Delay backstroke streamlines until level 3, or significant comfort exists with going underwater upsidedown.

Wrapped thumb

- Locking thumb keeps the hands together when pushing off or diving in.
- Locking also makes it easier to squeeze the ears. Press into thumb.

Behind the head?

- Some streamline with elbows pushed together behind the head. We feel it is important to use targeting language. Squeeze the ears gives a goal to press against.

Look up

- On backstroke look up instead.
- Face aims same as belly.

Lock your thumb

Pancake your hands, and wrap the top thumb around the bottom palm.

Lock it in by hooking your thumb and putting pressure against your other hand.

Many kids will say "lock your thumbs" with an "s." Can you lock the second one?

Locking the thumb holds them together when you push off and keeps them pressed firm when diving in.

Grown into a streamline by locking the thumb immediately.

Squeeze your ears

Press the elbows against the skull, or the back of the head. We say "squeeze your ears" to give swimmers a tangible body part to target.

We want them thinking about their arms pressing against their head, squeezing, putting pressure on their skull. It provides a tactile response and if they do this they're likely to lock their thumb and look down.

Use the whole arm and attempt to keep it straight. Elbows should not be bent unless starting to push from off the head into the streamline position.

Look down

Aim the entire face down, or in the same direction as the belly button.

Some swimmers will "look" down with their eyes only. Make this distinction clear and draw a circle around your face and say "aim your whole face down."

It make take repeated instruction and different approaches to get swimmers to orient their head down. Many like to look where they're going. Build a habit of not watching where you swim.

Front Crawl Arms - Freestyle

Begin with large circles ignoring what the hand does.

Start and finish every arm circle in Position 11.

The most familiar stroke is "Freestyle" or the front crawl.

Begin doing big arm circles with your swimmers when they are doing supported front glides. You can physically take their hands and move them in a large circular motion accounting for the way their shoulder flexes.

Allow a slight body roll to paddle arms in circles.

Ignore worrying about the hand; whether it cups, scoops, or has wide fingers does not matter. We care more about the general arm motion and the macro movement than we do the fine details.

Many instructors that already know how to swim get distracted by creating pretty, or beautiful arm strokes. Avoid this trap.

Teach straight arm circles first and later chip away at the details and how to do a high elbow recovery. For beginners we care about the concept of "pushing" the water backwards or under the body to move the person forward.

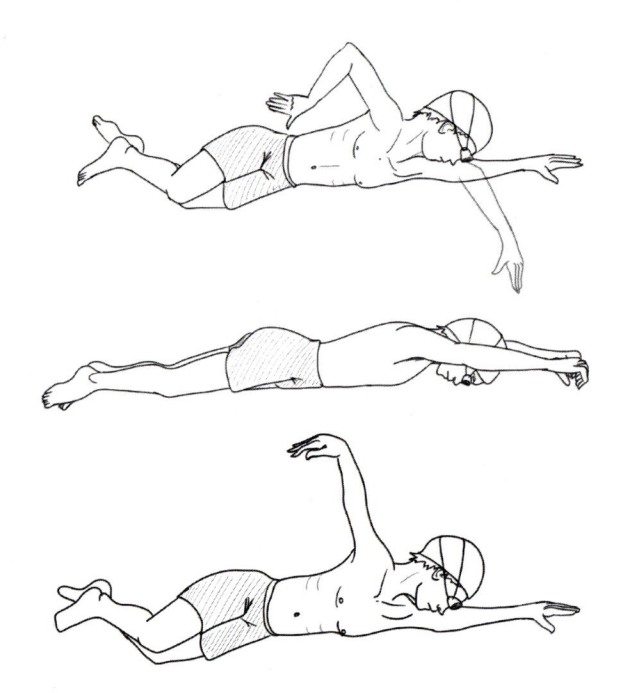

Begin teaching front crawl arms without breathing.

Do short distances where swimmers will have no need or direction to breathe.

We want swimmers to learn that the arm motion, the pull, moves their body through the water in addition to the kick.

Once arms are moving in large motions over the body with a gentle body roll and breathing is natural without struggling begin introducing a high elbow recovery with fingers and thumbs swinging wide in a semi-circle fashion.

Drag the forefinger and thumb across the top of the water from hips to position 11 drawing an arch or half circle.

High Elbow; top

- See pictures above. Arm returns to position 11 above the water with hand below the elbow. Arm swings like a compass.

- Slight body roll with each stroke.

Position 11; middle

- Exaggerate position 11 swimming to begin with.

- Remove long pauses in position 11 by increasing stroke rate.

- Encourage long reaches.

Straight arm; bottom

- Start with straight arms going over the water.

- Easier to teach and learn.

Swing wide through airplane

Begin teaching freestyle arms while standing on the deck. Start and finish each stroke in position 11.

Initiate an early forearm pull/push down by bending the elbow.

Rotate the hand out to airplane and return to position 11.

A wide recovery back to 11 is better on deck. In the water it will translate into a high elbow recovery.

Goal is to teach arm swinging around instead of zipping up next to the rib cage.

Finish near the hip and go

All pauses should be in position 11. Avoid letting the hands pause near the hips. Once the hands get to the waist then throw immediately over the water back into position 11.

Beginners: allow wide circles where hands swing above the elbow and shoulder. Body should roll with each stroke slightly no more than 45 degrees to surface.

Advanced: Drag fingers along surface in an arch, making sure that the elbow remains lifted. Avoid zippering next to the ribs.

Start with straight arms

For beginners start with large macro motions. Encourage circles or wide arms that do not bend.

Avoid talking about the hands. Let them push the water but refrain from talking about "ice cream scoops" or cupping fingers. This is an unnecessary step for beginners.

Aim your attention at teaching the arm recovers, or goes back to position 11 over the water and then in the water it pushes down, and behind the swimmer to provide forward motion. Do what you can to teach that pushing the water one way makes you move another.

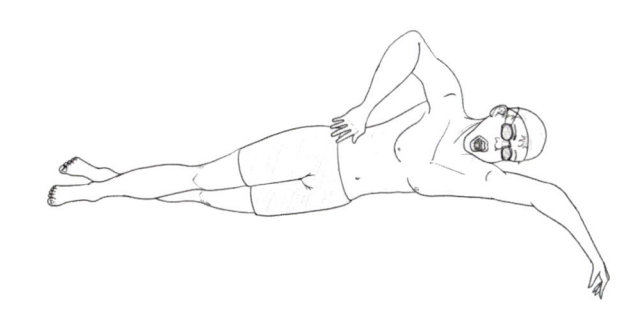

Start teaching arms during supported front glides.

Progress with supportive variations.

Aim attention at pushing water.

Teaching freestyle arms is like any other part of swimming; introducing an arm motion and then having your swimmers do it multiple times to learn the muscle memory that goes along with the movement.

Swimming is like dance choreography. We move our arms and legs in a coordinated fashion to present a specific dance or result.

Have your swimmers stand on the deck doing front crawl arms together. Have them do a low number of reps with good quality before you get in the water.

Begin in position 11 with arms reaching to the ceiling. Do one arm at a time and go slow, focusing on arms that reach tall with straight elbows above the crown of the head.

Even with swim team kids, who know how to swim freestyle well, if we give them 10 or 20 freestyle arms while standing on the deck they'll do sloppy bent elbow flops instead of slow deliberate movements.

Doing arm circles while swimmers wait in the water is questionable at best.

Many beginners are already in chest deep water. Doing arm circles while remaining on a bench or in shallow water without falling over is difficult. The water resists movement.

Avoid doing arm circles in place while the majority of the body is in the water.

Watch a swim instructor "demonstrate" front crawl arms while they're in waist deep water. Do they keep their arms in perfect position? Do they recover above their head as if they were laying in the water?

Practice free arms on the deck or horizontal in water.

Demonstrate well
- Do exactly what you want your swimmers to do. If you're sloppy with your arm demonstration your swimmers will be sloppy too.

Fewer Reps
- Limit arm circle practice to 3-5 reps, or arm strokes while on deck or in a supported glide.
- Encourage return to straight elbow position 11.

More "sets"
- Do 5 good free arms on deck 4 times throughout your lesson. Instead of 20 all at once.

24

Hands on Shoulders Free arms

Swimmer puts hands on the instructor's shoulders. Instructor should have shoulders in the water.

Walk backwards. Move one arm at a time. Tell swimmer to put hands back on your shoulders.

"Push the water down and back, then come around over the water back to my shoulders."

Physically move the swimmer's arms if they lack understanding or ability to do correctly on their own.

This is the first step to teaching muscle memory arm strokes.

Hands held by hands FR arms

Begin holding the swimmer's hands in your hands. Keep the arms and head near the surface of the water.

Walk backwards, pulling the swimmer.

Encourage kick. Encourage head down.

Tap, or push one hand to initiate an arm pull/circle.

Require swimmer to recover over the water and return to your hand.

Hold in as close to position 11 as possible.

Short swim 1st, then support

Start close; maybe 3 feet away or 1m. Have swimmer glide to you, grab their hands and do the "hands held by hands" support.

Instructor should plant themselves in a specific spot. Stay there until the swimmer gets to your position.

DO NOT BACK AWAY as they swim towards you.

Begin close, about 1 body length glide and another body length of arm strokes away. Increase distance away as swimmer comfort increases.

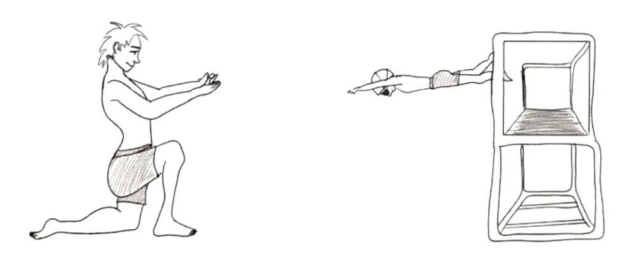

Freestyle Breathing

Turn head to side, look down. Avoid lifting at all costs.

Limit distance of swims to provide safe environment for low cost breathing attempts.

Breathing in freestyle is one of the more difficult things to teach and there are a variety of tactics to get swimmers to rotate their heads to the side, inhale, then place their face back in the water.

Like everything else, we feel that repetition, habit, and a safe encouraging environment is the best way to learn this complicated skill.

Remove the fear about breathing by starting with short distances that your swimmers are already comfortable with based on your previous glides and arm strokes.

Start introducing a breath to the side with strict adherence to only rotating head to the side without lifting on distances about 3 body lengths. The first body length should be a glide or streamline, then begin kicks and arms and do at least 1 breath during the swim.

Our goal is to remove as much fear and anxiety about breathing or getting water in your mouth or lungs as possible. Requiring a single breath on a distance well traveled and comfortable will help.

Avoid teaching side glide. There are programs that will tell their beginners to roll on their back or side with one arm extended to breath.

DO NOT DO THIS. When the swimmer moves on to swim team they require extensive re-training and we find that swimmers that never experience this "side-glide" format perform better quicker.

Teach turning the head to the side when the arm begins pulling underwater. Take the breath, make it quick, and by the time the arm recovers above the head the face should rotate back underwater.

Use short distances at first to ensure that the breath is quick. Turn to the side, breathe, turn down.

Start short

- Do 6 x swim bench to bench with a streamline and arm strokes. Must take 1 breath
- Distance should be about 3 - 4 body lengths.

Repetition, habit.

- Like all swimming we are teaching a habit, a choreography, a movement requiring specific adherence to form. Demand head to the side then back down.

Side Glide = Fail.

- Doggy paddling on your side or back is not freestyle breathing. Do not do it.

Standing Head Turns

Begin standing on the deck. Turn only the head to the side. Aim face forward, turn chin over one shoulder. Do it 10 times each shoulder.

Can also do standing in the water.

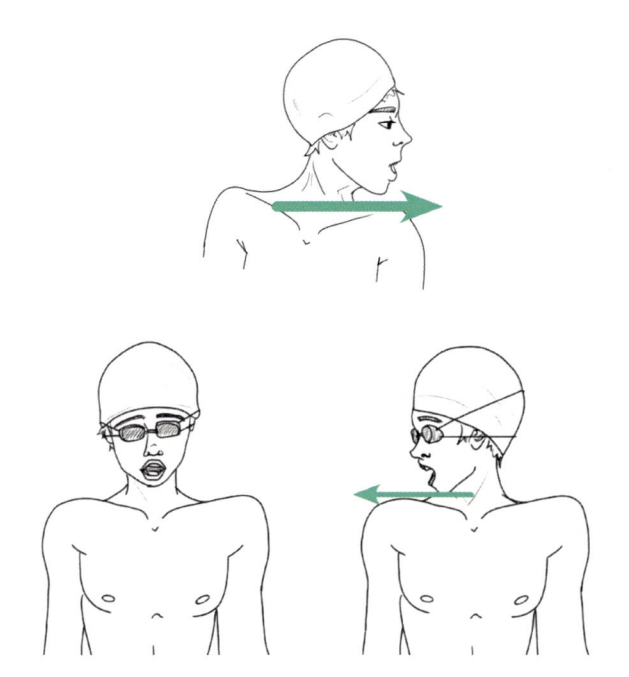

Stand in soldier position, look forward, then look over one shoulder. Repeat. Go slow.

As swimmers improve introduce a step back with the breath to the side while standing on deck. Breathe to right, take a half step back with right foot. Simulates body roll when swimming.

In water face down, side, down

Have swimmers stand in shallow water. Waist deep is best. Encourage bending knees and flattening back so it is flat in water.

Avoid letting swimmers float or not stand. Defeats the controlled nature of this activity.

Put only face in, then turn face to the side keeping back flat and near the surface.

When to the side keep 1/2 of face in the water. Breathe in, then immediately turn face to look down again. Go SLOW! Control body, control back, head.

Do shallow enough to keep back at the surface; about waist deep

Short distances, 1 breath

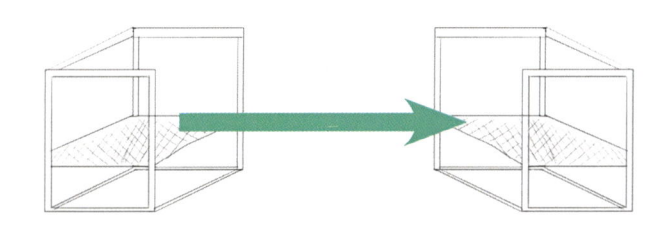

After breathing to the side is introduced have swimmers go from one bench to another with a glide, some arms and at least one breath to the side.

Keep distance short to alleviate anxiety, to make the breath a low struggle, easy attempt without panic.

Most beginners will struggle with the side breath and fear choking on water or not getting enough air.

Remove the complications by keeping swim short at first. Glide, arms, one breath. About 3-4 body lengths.

Freestyle breathing continued.

Long body with arms reaching to 11.

Quick breaths, avoid panting.

Short distance, remove fears.

We do not recommend practicing breathing to the side while doing supported front crawl arms, where the instructor is holding the child's hands or doing the hands on shoulder support.

Swimmers that breath while being supported tend to bend their elbows, rest their weight on the instructor and lift up instead of twisting their head to the side.

Doing short distance swims of about 3-5 body lengths or about 5 meters will remove fear.

Have swimmers complete swims with a breath the same distance they can already do without a breath.

If you don't have benches or shallow water, instructor can stand at distance away from the swimmer and 'catch' them when they arrive at your location. Stand directly in front of the swimmer, have them glide, then do arms and kicks to get to you. Pick them up by the arms and send them back.

DO NOT MOVE once they begin. Instructor should NEVER back away from a swimmer who is headed towards you. Once they put their face in the water you may not move.

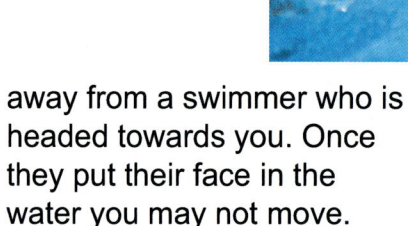

If you back away while they struggle to breathe you will destroy all of the trust they have in you and will create fear and anxiety.

If the distance away is too short then NEXT time back up.

There is a natural body roll to freestyle and breathing. This roll should not exceed 45° of the shoulders and hips to the surface of the water plane.

Breath should be quick near the beginning of the arm stroke and finished before the arm reaches above the swimmer's head and returns to position 11.

Side, Down, Side

- Turn to the side and attempt a breath.
- Okay to not breathe at first. Practice head turns.
- Immediate turn down after breath. No lifting up.

Breathe early

- Finish breath before arm reaches back over face.
- Quick breath at beginning of stroke easier.
- Non breathing arm stays in 11

Lips, Cheek, Eye

- Keep the corner of your lip, one eye, and whole side of face in water when breathing to the side.

One arm in 11, or position 1

We encourage you to do freestyle breathing with dramatic catch-up drill, or swimming in position 11, keeping one arm outstretched in front of head near surface in position 1.

When breathing to the side, rotate body, keep one arm outstretched, and breathe while the moving arm pushes the water behind swimmer.

A strong kick will help keep the body at the surface and allow an easier breath.

Head should only tun to the side when breathing.

Common mistake: Head up

Spend significant time and effort on correcting swimming with the head looking forward, or raised up so that the crown of the head points to ceiling or sky.

Place objects on the ground to look at, tap their head, or manually adjust head position.

Reinforce frequently with constant feedback: "put your head down, aim your face to the floor, push the water with the top of your hair like its a snow plow."

Many swimmers will look forward after a breath to the side. Create a new habit to stop it. Down, side, down.

Repetition, repetition, habit

Turning the head to the side to breathe is difficult. It will require a huge number of attempts to learn and do well.

Start with short distances building on the habits you've already taught like flat body posture, strong kick, position 11 and long reaching arms.

Have swimmers do short swims that they can do without needing to breathe and require 1 attempt at a side breath. Give critique and feedback on the breath to improve ability. Do lots and lots of attempts to learn.

Worksheet and Discussion #2

1) Describe how a flutter kick begins and what moves.

2) What are the three key points to streamline? What is the Streamline Script?

3) Is it difficult for young children to do a perfect streamline? Why or why not?

4) What language would you use to describe or instruct someone who has never swam to do freestyle arms on deck?

5) At first what will provide the most forward movement for beginners to freestyle? **Arm strokes** or **kicks**

6) What is soldier position?

7) What is position 11?

8) For beginners should you worry about how the elbow bends or if the hands are cupping or scooping the water?

Discussion topic #1: Side glide

Notes:

Side glide promotes doggy paddle, panting breathing where swimmers take 2 -4 breaths.

We can teach rolling on your back to breathe as a safety skill, as a option for survival or peace of mind.

Side glide is not an effective way to teach breathing to the side for freestyle. We can teach rolling on the back to swimmers that are comfortable putting their face underwater and doing back glides.

What would you have to retrain for someone that learned to side glide when taking a breath for FR?

Discussion topic #2: Short?

Notes:

Why is it better to do short distances with swimmers learning freestyle breathing?

Why do we demand you not move once a swimmer starts their swim towards your location?

How can we remove fear and anxiety about not being able to breathe when teaching freestyle?

Is there a place for longer swims with support, perhaps holding a kickboard and swimming freestyle a whole 25?

Discussion topic #3: Pretty

Notes:

If we want excellent freestyle and don't want to retrain someone why not teach high elbow recovery, scooping hands and early forearm down pulling?

Do you feel like encouraging straight arm circles for beginners starting freestyle is wrong? Why?

Should the hand enter the water near the face then extend forward in the water to position 11?

How splashy should freestyle be for beginners?

Backstroke Arms

Keep body straight, near surface.

Arms recover straight, elbow locked.

"Thumb, Hi, Pinky, Push"

Push with circle, then bend elbow.

Like freestyle arms we start backstroke with a good foundation in proper body posture.

Practice back stroke arms on the deck first.

Stand in soldier position with hands at hips.

Lift one arm in front of body width thumb aiming up.

When hand gets above shoulder, and head, rotate thumb so that it aims the same direction as the belly button.

Continue circle to return with hand at hip.

Optionally can demonstrate with bent elbow and the push, but this is advanced technique and not required for beginners to get the general motion.

Swimming backstroke can be frightening for beginners so provide support by holding the head and moving the arms for the swimmer.

Hold on the wrist just above the hand and lift thumb out of the water, rotate at the apex of recovery and enter the water with the pinky finger. Push water to the side and towards feet. Do next arm.

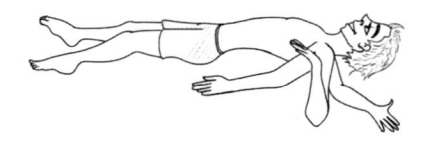

Focus on keeping the body and feet near the water and making sure that the face does not fall underwater too.

Most beginners will be hesitant to do the arms because they don't want to sink underwater and get water up their noses.

Ensure comfort on back with lots of glides doing support.

When transitioning to unsupported back glides hold off on doing arm strokes until swimmer has confidence to kick and keep body up near the surface without falling underwater.

Thumb

- When hands are at the hips lift the thumb out of the water first.
- Keep elbow straight when initiating the above water portion, or recovery.

Hi

- At the top of the recovery, when the hand is perpendicular to the belly rotate the hand, or wave "hello" to people on side of pool.
- Palm rotates out at apex.

Pinky

- Enter the water in position 11, near head with the pinky finger.

Supported arms

Hold the swimmer's head in your palm, keeping distance between their head and your chest.

Grab the swimmer's arm at the wrist and lift up, twist for "hi" and enter the water near your shoulder with the swimmer's pinky.

Push the water to this hips. Do other arm. Go one arm at a time.

Focus on keeping the swimmer's head supported and above the water. Teaching form, habit, and the feel of arms moving in correct direction.

Sloppy strokes at first

At first swimmers will have thrashing splashy arm strokes. The elbow will be bent when recovering, the kicks will be large and ineffective. The head and body position might be floppy and chaotic.

Put every effort into getting the body position and head correct first, then the feet.

Lastly refine the arm stroke. Straighten the arm as it travels above the water.

Encourage a bent elbow push to the hips. Provide support where needed and give feedback to improve.

Strong Kicks

If the kick is strong from your practice doing glides then you'll have a good solid body line at the surface that keeps the hips and head above water when the arms travel in the air.

Lifting your hand above your body when swimming causes the body to sink. Prevent falling underwater by keeping the kick strong.

Do lots of back glides with strong kick first before introducing back stroke without support.

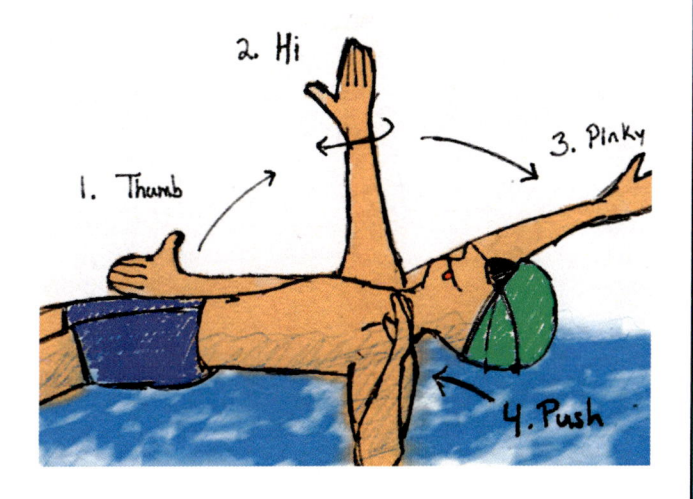

Back Crawl Arms:

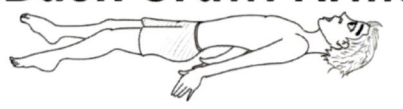

Body position 1st! train comfort & relax

Flat body line, belly near surface, head aiming up, ears in water.

Balance, learn head back feet up, attempt belly button high.

Be comfortable gliding on back using kick to move, knees low.

Thumb, "hi," pinky, push

Thumb lifts first out of water.

At apex, spin hand to wave "hi," palm out or away from belly.

Enter water with pinky first.

Anchor high in position 11.

Push/pull straight arm first, then bend elbow

Big circles best at first, ignore hands and bending until large "motion" is mastered.

Teach hand turning at height of reach 1st, then bent elbow pull.

Refine arm travel after comfort.

Body line, hip rotation

Hips and shoulders rotate with arms.

6 x glide on back 1/2 way, arm strokes 1/2.

Avoid pauses near hips keep arms moving.

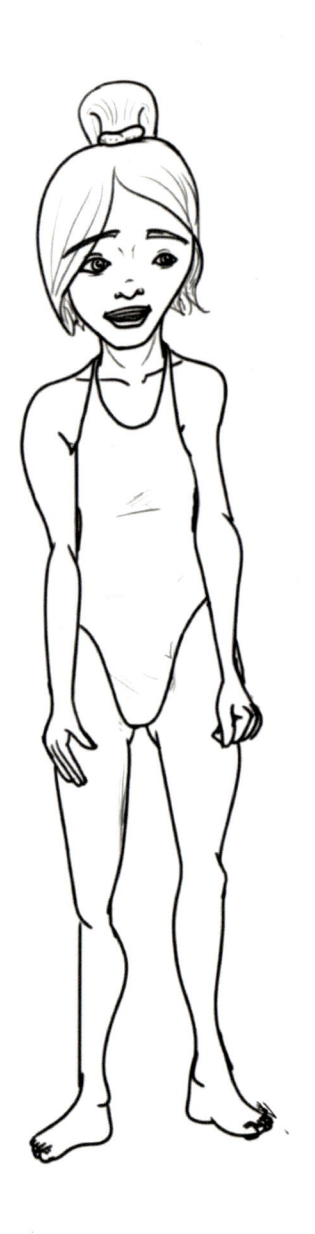

Start practicing backstroke arms in soldier position, pictured at left.

Lift arms forward in same direction as belly button.

There is a hip rotation to backstroke that will manifest as swimmers do their strokes and can be done on deck.

As the arm reaches above the swimmer's head, take a step back with that same foot, pivoting to make the arm stroke movement easier on the shoulder.

Many swimmers will get confused by which direction arms should move in doing freestyle arms or alternating arms in wrong directions.

Move swimmer's arms for them, corrected as needed.

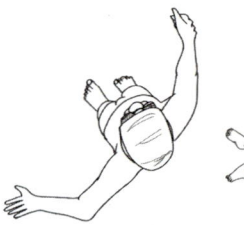

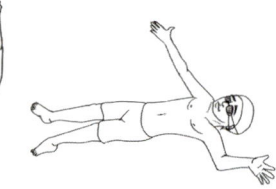

Straight Arms

- Begin teaching back arms with straight elbows.
- Aim for the large circle motion, then refine as habit gets direction and motion correct.

Refine with push

- Introduce bent elbow push by aiming fingertips to the walls. Right fingers point to right wall with each "push"
- Slap the thigh at the end of each "push." Lift thumb out of the water to recover.

Add hip rotation

- Rotating the hips makes arm strokes easier.
- HLBw/R drill to teach it.

Common Mistake: Poor Kick

If the swimmer is not kicking the heavy weight in the legs will drag the feet underwater. Keep the kick strong and effective so that the body remains in alignment at the surface of the water.

Smaller kicks are better at keeping feet near surface. Too big of kicks are inefficient and will lead to issues like pictured to the right.

Encourage body flat, strong kick, and tight kicks without too much large splashing hammer style kicks with the heels. Constant, small, propulsive kick.

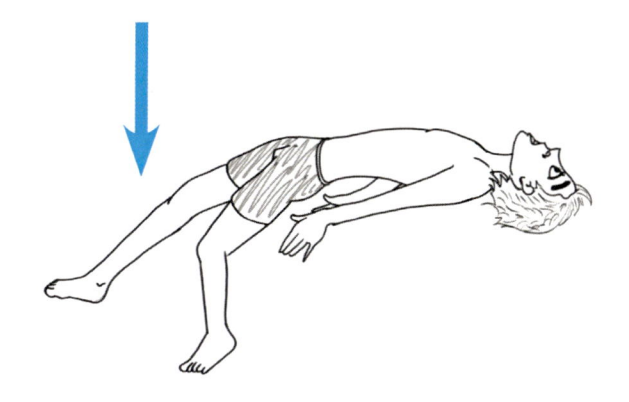

Common Mistake: Vampire neck

Along with a slow kick and a belly that pushes too high in the water a beginner swimmer may want to avoid getting water in their face by tilting their head too far backwards.

We want to push the water with the crown of the head, or top; the part you cover with a hat.

Don't let the neck stretch wide with lots of throat showing for a vampire to bite.

Ward off the pool vampires by hiding the neck with the chin by tucking it just a little bit.

Common Mistake: Wiggle Butt

This is very common in small children who lack the strength and the attention to keep their stomach squeezed and straight.

Adults that are uncomfortable will flail about as well.

Flatten out the legs with smaller kicks, keep the belly and trunk flat and narrow and avoid letting the butt swing to the sides with every stroke.

Wiggle butt often happens after introducing rotation. Keep body long and in soldier and kick narrow.

Breaststroke Kick

Lift
Flex
Circle
Push and Squeeze

FLEX:

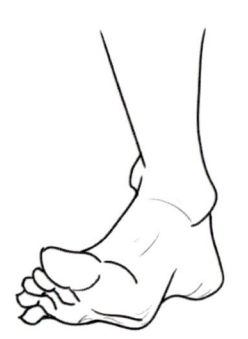

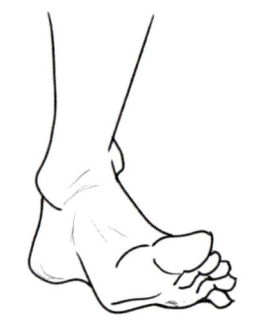

A segment of people have natural breaststroke kick. These are people that have learned intuitively the powerful force breaststroke kick can provide. You won't really need to "teach" breaststroke kick to them beyond refinement and gliding after each kick.

This section is for the majority of people that struggle with breaststroke kick.

Teaching the breaststroke kick, or the whip kick, is a slog, a long press through swampy struggle that will take significant patience, repetition, and focused feedback and refinement.

Do not be discouraged.

We've made it easier.

Begin with "flex." You'll notice it is the focal point on this page.

Put the feet together, rotate toes away from each other, then lift the big toes up.

Spend significant time introducing "flex" over and over. Establish the feet position as habit.

Breaststroke kick is a push and a squeeze that uses the inside of the foot.

Common mistakes are a fly kick, or a flutter kick where swimmers will be so used to using the top and bottom of their feet to push the water they do the kick wrong.

When swimmers start doing the breaststroke kick motion they'll often go very slow or not move anywhere. To compensate they'll do the kick wrong to provide motion.

Avoid this pitfall by restricting distance. Do short glides where swimmers do the kick motion.

Do a streamline with flex. Stop. Do a streamline with lift and flex. Stop. Do a full breaststroke kick, glide. Stop.

Lift and Flex

- Start in position 11 with feet neutral.
- Lift feet above the knees
- Flex the feet keeping knees close together.

Push, Squeeze

- Snap feet backwards and squeeze together.
- Press water with the inside of the feet.
- Water resistance will flare toes out to the sides.

One strong kick

- Kick then GLIDE. Let kick carry swimmer forward.
- Return to 11 and wait.

Sit on the side

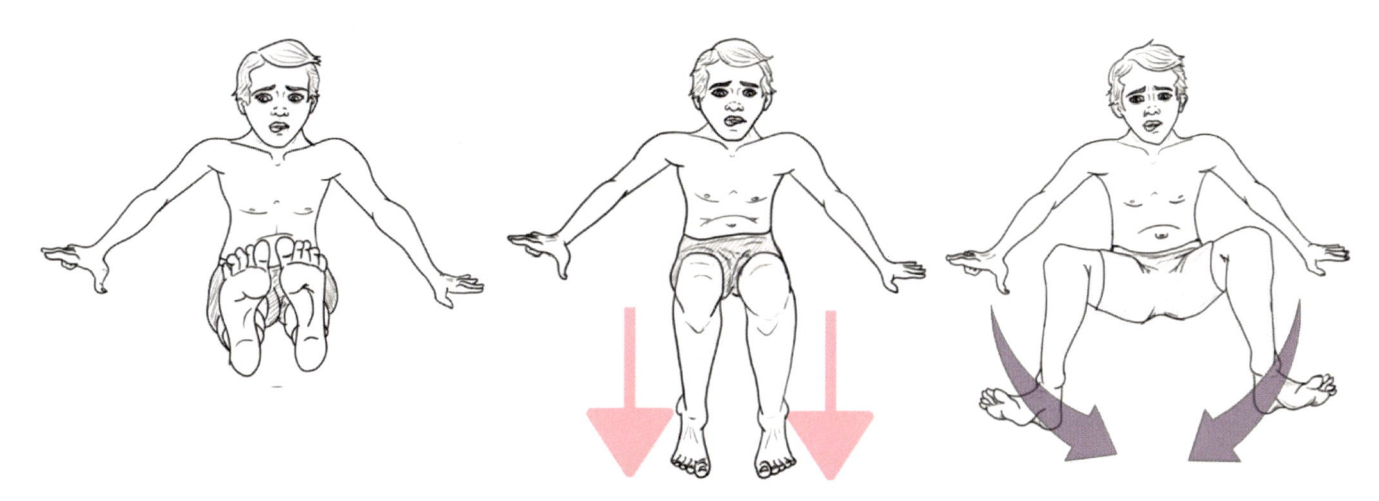

After practicing "FLEX" have swimmers sit on the side of the pool with only their butts resting on the edge.

May need to support body with hands out to the sides.

Extend the legs straight out away from the wall.

Bend the knees to put the heels/feet on the wall.

Flex toes outwards, so that both feet are pointing away from each other.

Make a circle and a squeeze while pushing the water with the inside of the foot returning to the original position with legs extended.

Kick progression in water:

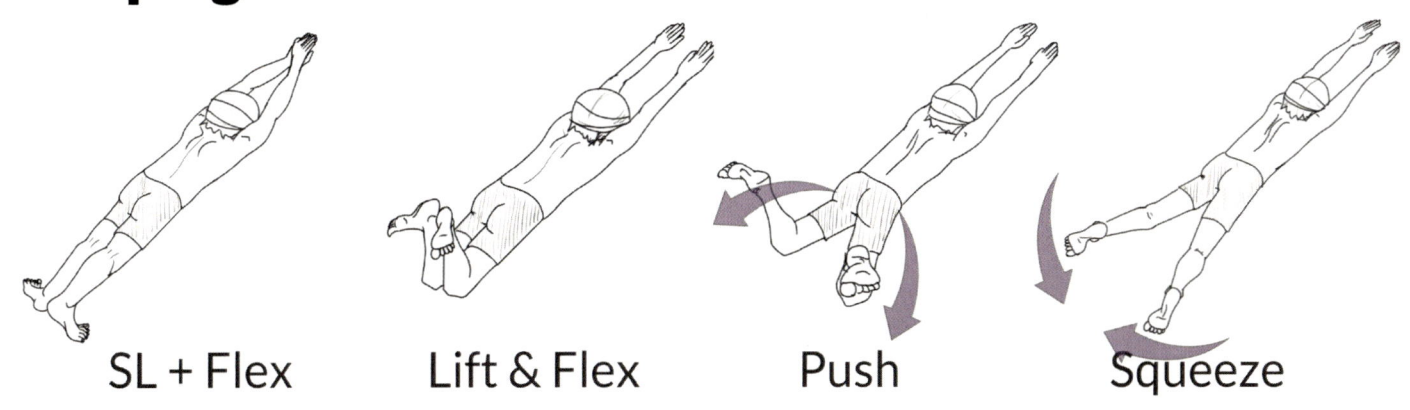

SL + Flex   Lift & Flex   Push   Squeeze

Breaststroke Arms

11, Eat, 11.

Avoid wide sweeping circles or pizza sauce wax on wax off movements.

Simplify.

Make breaststroke easier. Simplify your instruction.

Most beginners in Breaststroke get disqualified because they bring their hands past their hip-line, they "swim" with their arms sweeping in a wide circle like reverse butterfly.

We can make teaching this complicated, difficult, nuanced stroke easier.

It is easier to add a scull, or a sweep to a breaststroke arm stroke than it is to take away an excessive one.

To begin, our instruction will be entirely on the MOTION, or the choreography of the breaststroke arms and the kick before we care about propulsion or speed.

Master the limb movements and strength and the swim will come after.

Most or all of your instruction and exposure will be tied to a streamline with no kick, because there is no kick in breaststroke until the arms move first.

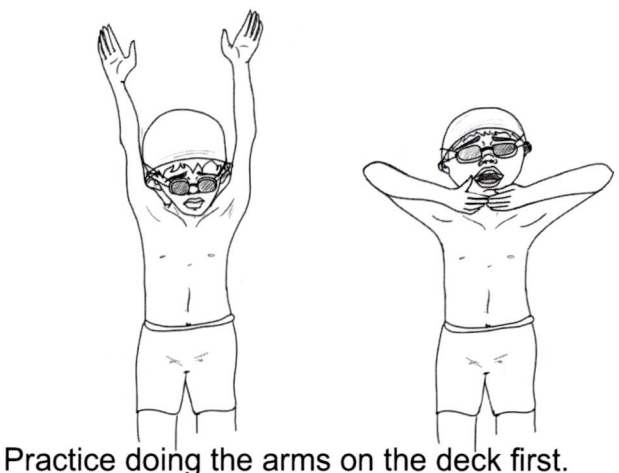

Practice doing the arms on the deck first.

5 x 11, Eat, 11. Go slow, keep head still.

Begin in 11.

Bend the elbows and push hands towards the face; Eat.

Return forward without embellishment to 11.

11, Eat, 11. The dance, the movement.

When that sequence is mastered add a breath.

11, Eat and Breathe, 11.

Go slow, take time, and enforce strict adherence to this specific motion. There is no "Y" or outward scooping sweeps to begin with.

Simply, 11, Eat, 11.

Allow swimmers to push water towards their face transitioning from 11 to Eat.

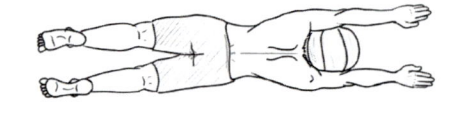

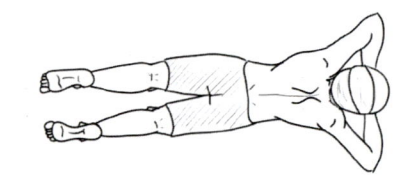

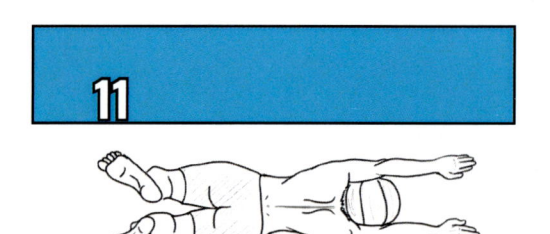

Repetition

Drill this motion into your swimmers. 11, Eat, 11.

Avoid rushing through this and avoid sloppy bent elbows in 11. Our goal is to establish a deliberate habit of careful precision.

Pause in 11 for a few heartbeats. Pause in Eat. Return to 11 and make it a deliberate hold.

Do this sequence at the beginning of your practice or lesson on the deck before you get in. Get out before doing breaststroke arms in the water and do on deck.

Reiterate that the arms will not make body move, yet.

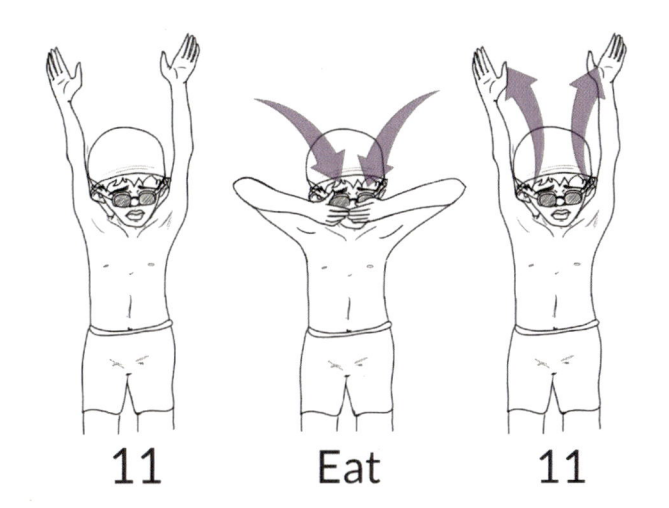

Glide, 11, Eat, 11, glide.

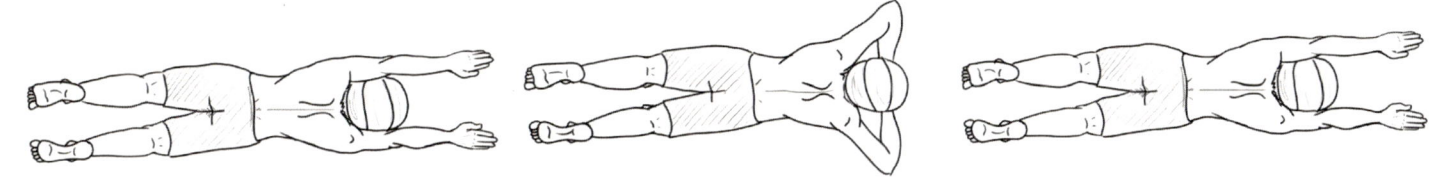

No kicking. Push off the wall. Glide in 11, do one "eat," and return to 11 and glide or float again.

We are doing the motion, the choreography, not actual pulling through the water and swimming, yet.

Adhere strictly to the specific series of movements. Be deliberate, avoid doggy paddle, wide sweeping arms, and flowery hand motions. Make it simple, make it slow, make it easy: 11, Eat, 11.

Mastery

After swimmers have a strong kick that propels them forward and they can do the timing of 11, Eat and Breath, 11, Kick, Glide, begin introducing the sweep/scull transition from 11 to Eat.

Once stroke basics are mastered introduce inward sweeping elbows on the recovery and the feet lifting as the head presses forward and back into streamline.

It is so much easier to add these "embellishments" than it is to chip away at bad habits learned from overzealous instructors teaching advanced BR arms.

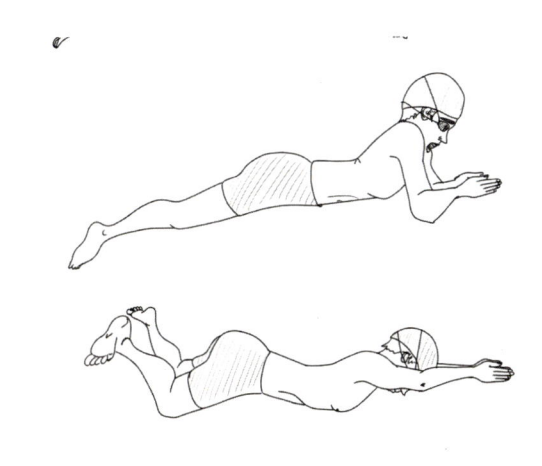

Worksheet and Discussion #3

1) What is position 11? Describe in detail, or draw a picture:

2) What is the script you'd use to introduce breaststroke arms to a beginner?

3) TRUE or FALSE : SL + Flex is an activity where there is no kick and the swimmer glides off the wall with toes turned apart and raised.

4) How will a "vampire neck" hurt a swimmer's backstroke?

5) "Thumb, Hi, Pinky, Push" describes what swim motion?

6) Should the chin be slightly tucked in when swimming backstroke?

Discussion topic #1: Rotation

Notes:

General recommendation is that backstroke and freestyle have a significant (~45°) hip and shoulder rotation that flows with the armstrokes.

Should we encourage this rotating with beginners?

How much explicit direction should we give new swimmers about rotating their hips while they swim?

What are some drills or activities that are not full swimming that you can do to teach hip rotation?

Can we get swimmers to rotate without telling them to?

Discussion topic #2: Dancing?

Notes:

11, Eat, 11 is a choreography, a dance move. We hammer into our swimmers the framework of breaststroke arms to remove issues and errors later on when swimming the stroke.

What is the benefit or downside of teaching this reduced bare-bones sequence of arm movements instead of "pretty" breaststroke arms?

How is swimming like dancing?

What mistake are we attempting to "head off at the pass" by teaching 11, Eat, 11 without care for propulsion? (forward movement in water by hands)

Discussion topic #3: Natural

Notes:

Some people have a natural intuitive breaststroke kick. What do we do with the other 90% that don't?

What are some common mistakes to breaststroke kick?

Should our emphasis be on "flexed" feet with rigid muscles, or should we encourage floppy out-turned toes to let the water push against the inside of the foot?

What is the benefit of SL + Lift and Flex?

Butterfly Kick

Undulation

Roll from the chest down through the toes.

Keep the head still.

Fly kick is a whole body motion that rolls through the chest and belly, down through the pelvis and thighs, and snapping down the knees and feet.

Undulation describes this "rolling wave" motion like a sine wave from mathematics. To undulate is to press the chest, the belly, hips and legs in a rolling hill like pattern.

It is best to keep moving when doing fly kick. Use the whole body with the arms at the sides in "soldier" position. Press with the chest, roll with the hips, and snap the feet up and down.

The whole body rolls like it is creating small waving mountains through the water.

Most swimmers, young and old, will learn fly kick best by watching someone do it, then attempting it on their own.

Challenge beginners to keep their head still and avoid using their arms with doggy paddles to help provide forward motion. Use the whole body to wiggle the body forward like a dolphin.

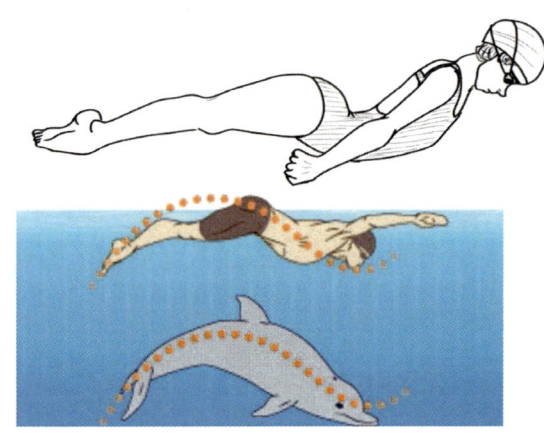

Key points:

Keep head still if possible. Some motion okay.

Feet should remain close together. Avoid letting feet spread apart too far (wider than shoulders).

Legs and feet should go up and down together, at the same time, in parallel.

Hips should drive most of the motion by flexing the quads and hamstrings as well as pinching the stomach.

Press the chest down and create a divot, or space, in the lower back. Chest down, hips up, then switch; hips down, chest retracted.

Keep rolling in constant motion.

Undulate = the wave

- Like doing the wave with arms in airplane, like mime, keep the chest, hips, and legs moving like the wave is traveling down your body from crown to toes.

Stable head

- Struggle to keep the head still. Let the fly kick start with the chest and roll down through the hips and legs.

- Initiate the "kick" from the chest. Press with the hips.

Dolphin strong

- Fly kick is powerful. Use your whole strength with core, legs, and back muscles all engaged.

Flowing kick

Like the picture to the side, the fly kick should be like rolling hills, or the "sine wave" while undulating through the water.

Think of the head or body mass as being the flat horizontal line. The hips and chest are the peaks and troughs, or the rolling up and down curved line.

Keep body in constant motion so that the kick flows through and in the water.

Hips can crest the surface but feet should not create too much splashing.

SINE WAVE

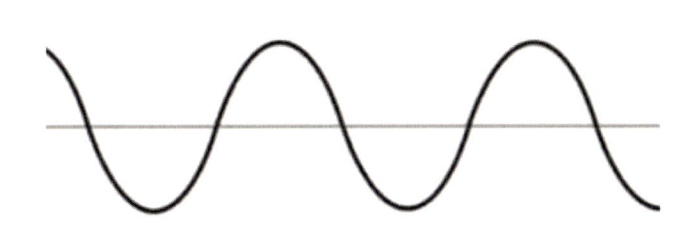

Fly kick in streamline is hard.

It requires significant flexibility in the back, which many don't have. Once fly kick with arms in position 11 is mastered, then introduce fly kick with streamline position.

Streamline is already difficult alone. Add fly kick with careful observation.

Begin with a streamline, as always, encourage the fly kick, but allow mistakes. Head will move often, arms won't be tight against ears. Provide feedback, but focus should remain on hands in soldier and the hip motion with feet moving in parallel.

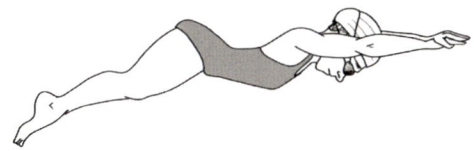

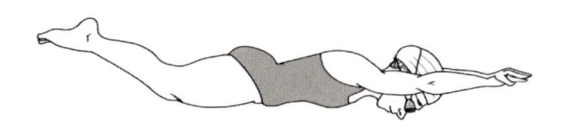

Chest press & Legs together

Most beginners will pick up the hip motion right away. Two points of difficulty are often the chest pressing down and retracting up and the feet moving together.

Beginners will have legs that fall apart, not moving at the same time, and independent splashing.

They'll also forget to use their chest and instead use their head to drive the kick motion.

Talk often about stabilizing the head and moving the legs together, in parallel, close together for good kicks.

Butterfly Arms

Let the body motion lift your shoulders.

Sweep wide through airplane.

Extend all the way forward to 11.

Fly is a powerful stroke. Yes, the arms are difficult, full of power, and can be exhausting. But if you do the motions correctly, well, and with fluid grace you can easily do lots of butterfly swimming.

Problems rise when swimmers try to muscle their way through FLY and ignore the kick.

The fly motion is relatively simple, done exactly the same on deck as it should be in the water.

Your challenge will be to get swimmers to go through the fly arm motions slowly while standing then translate that same swinging ease into the water.

Spend significant time reviewing butterfly arms while standing. If you can use mirrors in a studio or big window that reflects do so.

Most swimmers will try to lift their arms above the water, extending their shoulders back, and hands up in the air like wings, or like they think freestyle looks like.

Butterfly is an outwards swing with arms at full extension.

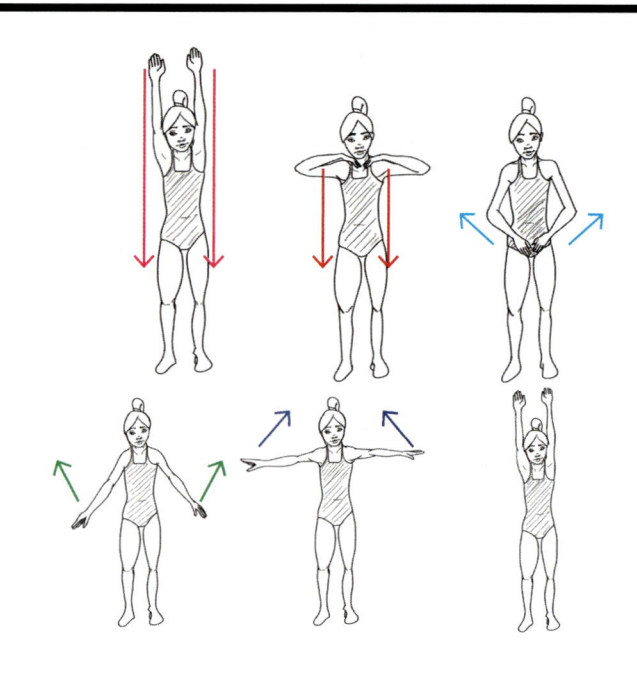

On deck, key points:

- Begin in 11.

- Push the hands down to the hips as if doing two simultaneous freestyle strokes.

- Flare out into airplane position. Elbows locked.

- Clap the back of your hands above your head returning to position 11.

In water key points:

- Do the motion first without need to "swim" forward.

- Arms stay near surface.

- Aim thumb the same direction as belly button.

- Return to 11

Airplane
- Aim thumbs same direction as belly button. Palm down.

Clap the back
- When going from 'airplane' into position 11 to complete the fly stroke have beginners "clap" the back of their hands above their head. This tactile cue will help target the motion.

Straight elbows
- Under the body bend.
- Coming around back to 11, keep them straight.

Go SLOW!

Lead fly arms on the deck by making sure participants keep their arm motions slow matching your pace.

Start in 11. Push both arms down for butterfly.

At the hips, sweep out and extend to airplane.

Keep thumbs aiming same direction as belly button whole time on the way up.

Clap the back of your hands above your head.

Return to position 11.

No kick, 1 fly motion in water.

Once mastery on deck is demonstrated begin repetitions in the water.

Glide with no kick in streamline. At the surface do 1 fly arm motion. Do the movement, not trying to "swim."

Push water down to your toes. Stop at your suit (where it ends or begins) and draw a circle with your thumbs on the surface aiming your thumbs to the bottom of the pool.

Palm, hand, elbows rise just above the surface of the water. Clap the hands above the head in 11, pause.

Hands in 11, butt up.

Combining the arms and the kick is problematic and challenging. Overcome this irritating skill by reinforcing this mantra: when the arms are in 11, the butt is above the water.

The hips should pop up when the arms reach to extension at position 11.

Practice by pulling hands to swimsuit start/end and pushing hips forward. Return to 11 and thrust hips back, sticking butt backwards like a gymnast pose after the parallel bar dismount. Hands up, butt up.

Flip turns

Flips in water 1st.

Breath control; bubbles through nose.

Controlled rolling.

Flip turns are when you swim at the wall in freestyle and backstroke, do a front flip, plant your feet on the wall and push off in streamline on your back.

They are difficult and intimidating because they rely on wide range of skills and comfort.

But we can make them easier and gradually introduce flipping to make it less intimidating.

Begin with flip attempts. Show swimmers what it is. Talk about how to blow bubbles with your nose, and encourage them to make an attempt.

Some will master it quickly. Others will struggle. Praise the attempts.

Move on to adding a flip to the end of your shorter swims. Do freestyle with no breath for 3 strokes then do a flip. See if you can do it without any breaths in between.

For more experienced swimmers have them do it in the middle of a length. Do flips during play time as rewards. Give 2 flip in 10 second challenges. Expose them to flips.

How to flip:

Lay on your belly. Have some small forward movement, like push off the wall in streamline.

Tuck your chin, and lift your butt. Your legs and body will carry over your core if you're tucked into a half ball.

Allow legs to flop over your head.

Really. It is that simple. If you're moving a little bit the momentum will carry the trunk and legs over the tucked head and crunched belly.

Feet should land on the wall near each other, but squared roughly with the shoulders.

Push off on your back in streamline. *Rotate over later.*

Chin tuck, lift butt

- If you're moving flips are easier. Practice small flips.
- Tuck your chin down.
- Lift your butt in the air.
- Keep your legs close.

A half-flip

- A flip turn is really going from your stomach to your back, flipping your feet and butt over your head.
- Like a 1/2 flip. Start on your stomach, land 2 feet on the wall, on your back.

Push off on Back

- No twisting on the wall.
- Land on your back, push off the wall on your back.

Unassisted flips

Allow swimmers to attempt a flip as early as level 2, or when they start going underwater on their own. Encourage them to close their mouth and talk while underwater; it will create bubbles.

This is a free-form, challenge based activity where you praise the attempt. Do this in shallow water participants have room to move around in and can fail with thrashing splashing arms.

Make this slightly more difficult by having swimmers do a handstand first, then turning it into a front flip.

Flips + [something]

Combine your flips with an activity to make it easier or more challenging. Here we are tethering the flip to motion to begin introducing the idea that you swim at a wall and flip when you get to it.

Do streamlines with kick that end in a flip.

Do streamline + 3 free strokes + a flip at the end.

Each flip should be an attempt with feedback to improve quality.

Do handstands for 2 seconds, then turn the handstand into a front flip.

Flip + foot targeting.

Do a glide from the "T" mark towards the wall. Flip aiming feet at the "+" sign, or the flip turn marker.

The feet should land on the wall near the horizontal line.

Practice getting the back flat. If the head is raised, or the back is bending forward the person flipped too far.

Practice targeting different areas on the wall with the feet to learn precision. Do 2 flips landing both feet above the horizontal line, on it, under it, etc.

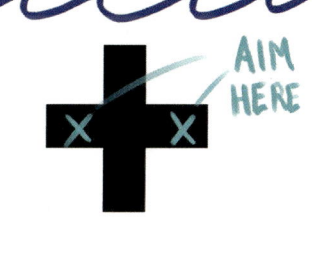

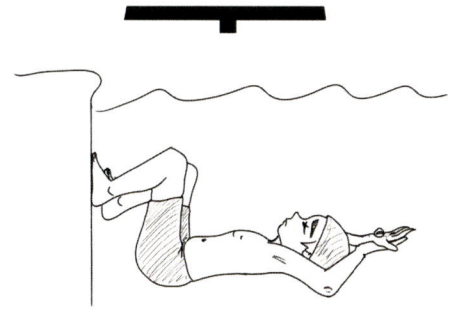

Open Turns

Begin slow. Move through steps deliberately.

Two hand touch.

Get on your side. Head is stable.

Open turns are for Breaststroke and Butterfly. They are the alternative to a flip turn.

The goal is to touch the wall with two hands underwater (not grabbing the edge of the pool) quickly pull the legs into the chest and push off on your side.

It can be a very quick racing turn if done well and with precision, but will take considerable time and practice to master.

Most people struggle by going too quickly, flailing their limbs, and not following the exact procedure to do the turn efficiently.

Most common mistakes are pulling up on the side of the pool, splashing the belly down at the wall, or pushing off on the back.

Like most other skills you should break up this turn into it's different pieces or chunks.

2 hand touch.

Pull feet in and press them to the wall. Get on your side, fall underwater, and push off on side.

Open Turn steps:

- Touch the wall with both hands on your belly. Head should be underwater.

- Tuck the knees into your chest as you pull into a ball and swing your feet against the wall. Twist body to land on your side. One hand remains on the wall.

- Pull one arm back like drawing a bow with an arrow, or elbow the person behind you. Keep hand close to body.

- Shoulders go perpendicular to the surface of the water.

- Head remains looking at the wall, then as body falls down, at the ceiling.

- Fall under on your side and push off in streamline.

Twist to your side

- After 2 hand touch, rotate to your side.
- Keep your face aiming at the wall.
- Pull knees under body and swing them at the wall

Throw elbow back

- Pull your elbow back behind you like drawing an arrow on a bow.
- Twist elbow to put hand on your head.
- Fall backwards and down.

Karate Chop

- Slap yourself in the head with the hand that was grabbing the wall. Fall underwater.

Look at the wall, Ring the Bell

Elbow the person behind you with one elbow.

Throw it back keeping your arm close to your chest while you twist sideways.

Legs should bend and tuck in, swinging like a pendulum under the shoulders.

The head should remain focused on the wall with the chin over the shoulder which is holding on.

Feet should land on the wall stacked on each other, and butt should rise up towards the surface after swinging under the body.

Karate Chop, Aim face up

Once the feet are planted, rotate the "elbow jammed backwards" and put hand on head preparing for a streamline.

The hand that was on the wall bends at the elbow, and "karate chops" yourself in the face.

Make this "karate chop" as quick, small, and fast as possible.

Allow body to fall directly down with the face aimed up throughout.

Head will fall back so that body lays on side for SL.

Fall down and streamline

Let the body fall down underwater, rotate head to look at the bottom of the pool and push off on your side.

Begin rotating immediately on to the belly.

Initiate the push off on your side.

Minimize rotation, twisting, or laying on the belly before pushing off the wall.

If possible aim the head down to the bottom of the pool before you fully leave the wall.

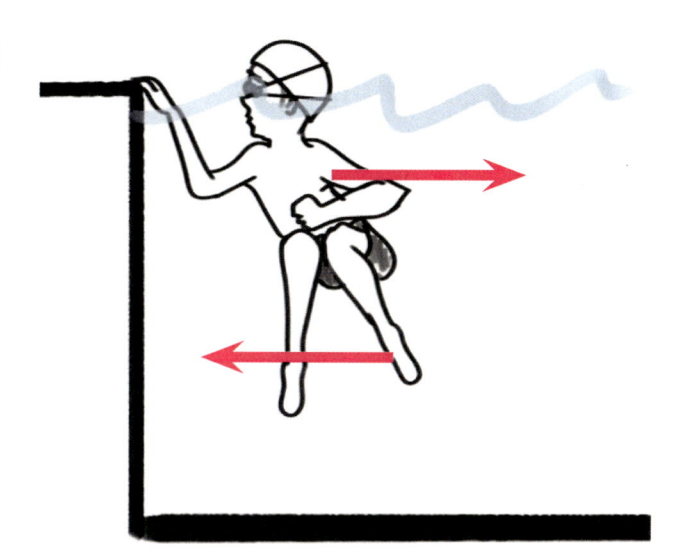

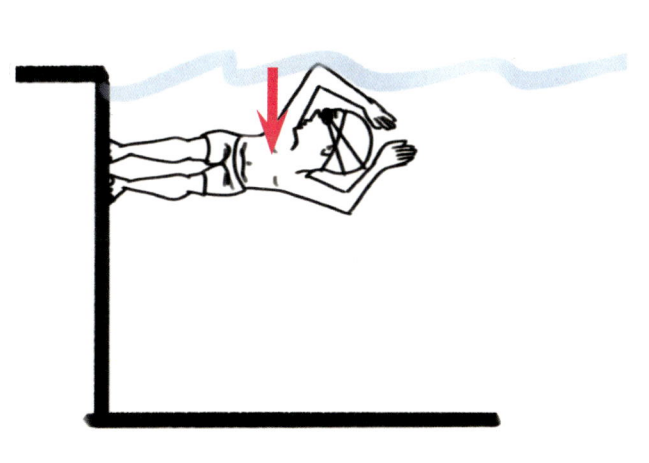

Worksheet and Discussion #4

1) What aquatic animal can we talk about to describe butterfly kick?

2) What is "undulation?" Describe in detail:

3) What are two things you can tell a swimmer to do to make a front flip easier?

4) When swimming fly should the hips or butt rise above the surface with the kick when the arms are in position 11?

6) TRUE or FALSE   When doing a flip turn you should push off on your back and rotate to your belly during the streamline while you are *not* touching the wall.

7) Open turns are for what two strokes? What is the first step?

Discussion topic #1: Fear

Notes:

Going underwater and doing supported front glides and back glides can be terrifying.

What are some elements of swim lessons that might be scary for a new participant?

Do those fears change or become more expressed based on the age of the swimmer?

What are infants afraid of?

What about toddlers (2-4 years old)?

What are 5+ afraid of?

Discussion topic #2: Underwater

Notes:

Should we dunk our swimmers?

Have you heard the phrase "sink or swim?" Do you have an experience with being tossed in the water and forced to either survive or sink to the bottom of the water?

Does throwing someone that doesn't know how to swim provide a benefit?

What are the positives of gentle, loving, gradual encouragement over throwing someone in without help?

Discussion topic #3: Floats

Notes:

Should you do floats before glides?

We skipped floats deliberately. Why?

What are the benefits of teaching stationary floating?

Can you achieve the same goals with skipping straight to glides?

Is there any value to teaching horizontal forward progress or motion over stationary floating?

How to teach: Method and Delivery

Knowing what to teach is the first step outlined in section 1.

How we conduct our instruction is just as important.

In section 1, we walked you through the 15 essential swimming skills. You should have a good understanding of each of the main swimming skills so you can teach them.

Use the training sheets at the back of this book, or included by your trainer while in the water. Reference the SwimSheets or lesson plans available on our website for further resources.

As a beginner swim instructor, there is no expectation that you will have memorized every single progression and all of the specific scripts.

Instead, we want to expose you to all of the skills. The goal is for you to see the incremental progression as one step leads into another.

We start with underwater so we can do glides, then add kicks so we can practice arms, and finally breathing.

Look at every swimming stroke, Fly, Back, Breast, and Free. How can you break them up into digestible chunks like cutting a steak or a piece of chicken?

Most new swim instructors will start with the very little beginners, toddlers and kids that don't go underwater.

Our swimming foundation is "going underwater," and on that, we build glides and horizontal forward motion.

Remember that the primary focus for most of swim lessons is going to be a straight long bodyline and core that looks a lot like soldier position. Consider how to incorporate "soldier" position into all of the swimming strokes.

Soldier Position: stand with spine as straight as possible. Head should rest squarely over torso, chin pushed back into the neck but not down or up, but back. Shoulders should be loose but slightly raised and pushed just behind ears. Pull your tummy in without holding your breath and tilt or rotate hips slightly forward as if pressing your tail-bone to the floor.

With section 2, we are going to show you HOW to teach all of those skills. While you can use section 1 as your only source of swim instructor training by literally walking through the 15 essential swim skills and using those progressions to teach your classes, we want to cover some more specific things that make okay teachers into awesome super +1 swim instructors that their students talk about all the time. Following these swim lesson specific teaching instructions will make you a better teacher overall and give you stronger confidence outside the pool.

We're going to cover topics like the language you use.

Do you know why you shouldn't say the word "Okay" at the end of a sentence?

We'll look at how you can set up your class area accounting for different pool formations.

Would you put your 3 year olds in the deep end forcing them to hold onto the wall while they waited for their turn?

We'll discuss how you should actually hold swimmers, including infants, so that you're prepared when you start teaching a "Parent and Baby" class.

Would you dunk an infant by dropping them in the water after tossing them in the air?

We'll look at how you should speak with a voice full of command that immediately drives your swimmers into action. They'll snap to attention at your voice because you'll learn how to instill respect and compliance. Let's go!

Section 2 is broken into 5 categories:

1) Communication

2) Class Organization

3) Lesson Plan Preparation

4) How to Hold swimmers

5) How to handle going underwater

Deliberate words
- What you say matters! Even down to the pauses, filler words, and hesitation how we speak directly influences how others perceive us. Learn to speak with command!

Be prepared
- Set up your class area in advance. Have your toys, materials and props ready before your swimmers arrive.
- Know where to go and what to do before you start

Be confident
- Provide support without making your swimmers more afraid.

Discussion Items:

What are some things people do when speaking publicly that make you question their authority?

What about their competence?

Can you think of a sentence where the way you say it changes the meaning even though the words are the same?

What are some basic materials you can gather before you swim lesson so that you can use them during your class?

If you forgot something and it is out of the water how would you go about getting it while still providing a safe environment for your swimmers?

Using Command Language

Speak with calm confidence resting on your experience and knowledge.

Use lesson plans to know exactly what to do.

Examples of Command Language:

"Ok, we're going to do this three times: streamline then do 3 freestyle strokes. Streamline ½ way, and use the 3 strokes to get you the other half to the bench. Any questions? Ok, go."
"Mary, we're going to do three jumps. Are you ready? Ok, Go!"
"Johnny, go underwater 3 times."
"Billy, we're doing a front glide. Ready, Go."

Command language is essential for beginning swim instructors to use because it is a simple way to establish authority and control over swim classes without doing anything extraordinary or too difficult. Commands give clear goals, expectations, and directions to a large group of people effectively.

Look at swimming lessons on a basic level:

Swimming can be fatal.

We are going to teach people to move their bodies in extremely specific motions that they are not comfortable doing on their own, or have never done before.

The participants may not want to do what we are attempting to teach them, may be afraid of what we want them to do, and will attempt to follow our directions and likely fail needing correction.

The swim instructors need to establish authority, dominance, and control over their students/participants in order to ensure a safe, productive, fun class.

We need to give clear instructions. We expect those instructions to be carried out by our participants because if they are not the swimmer may inhale water, drown, or cause a situation where others are in danger. This is an extreme example but it speaks to the serious potential for disaster that swimming has that other land based sports lack. Our instructions need to be carried out, not just because we are the swim teacher, but because we are organizing and conducting a class in a potentially fatal environment.

Our primary goal is to keep our swimmers alive and to teach them how to swim second. To do that, we should use commands and language of authority to organize the class, give directions, and provide feedback.

When we give clear commands to our participants and we say them in a way that give goals with alternate options of success, we create an environment where our participants expect to be told what to do, but have the freedom to carry out those commands however they can.

We want to give the participants limited options on how and what to do, but give them the sense of freedom to try new things. Do not mistake command language for authoritarian absolute dictatorships. We should expect to be listened to, but not dictate every motion and step a swimmer takes.

Example of a clear command with alternate choices:

"Billy, you're going to do 5 streamlines from this bench to the other bench. Each time you go from one to the other it is 1. You have 2 goals: 1) Look down while doing your streamline 2) kick your feet the whole time. Ready? Go."

In the example, the swimmer understands instinctively from the language that he can choose not to kick, or if he forgets because he is focusing on something else, that is okay. His GOAL is to go beyond the basics of a streamline and do a strong kick constantly, and be extra sure to look down. The command and instructions are clear and allow the swimmer to achieve the goal without extra specific steps on when to do each time, how exactly they should push off the wall, etc.

When you speak to your participants consider what you want to accomplish first. Be clear in what they will be doing, and give any extra instructions on how they can accomplish the task. If necessary, give modifications so everyone can achieve some success. As you will see in the next section, do not turn your commands into questions!

Command language does not mean being rude ordering your swimmers around as if they were hay wearing peasants and you were a feudal Queen.

Speak with confidence.

State what the group is going to be doing, define how you want it done, and tell them exactly what to do at each step of the way.

The more you give commands the more receptive to them your swimmers will become.

Start small with easily achievable objectives. "Sit here." "Do 5 kicks in the water." "Kiss the water 3 times or put your chin in 4 times."

Speak with ".'s"

- Remove question marks from your language.
- Speak in short sentences like you're learning a new language; your swimmers are!

Give praise

- Balance out your commands with lots of praise and encouragement when your swimmers do what you say; give high fives, verbal praise, or non-verbal thumbs ups.

Action words

- Tell your swimmers what to DO. Go here, move your arm this way, put your face in the water. Use verbs.

Discussion Items:

What is the primary goal of swimming lessons?

What are some examples of clear, concise commands?

Give an example of a command that also offers two stretch goals beyond the given task.

Example: *"Jonny, walk to the front of the classroom. While walking there you have two goals: 1) give 1 person a high five 2) jump once at least two inches into the air. Do you have any questions? Ok, go!"*

How would you instruct an alien to make a peanut butter sandwich? Remember to be as specific as possible, and assume nothing.

55

Remove "okay" from your sentences

Speak with periods at the end of your commands.

Be confident. You're in charge and they need to listen.

Read the following commands to see how they are turned into questions by adding "okay:"

"Johnny, go underwater 3 times, Okay?"

"Billy, we're going to a front glide, okay? Go."

Notice how adding the "okay" at the end of the sentence changes the statement into a question.

Read the next two sentences aloud:

"Billy, will you do a front glide?"

"Johnny, do a back float, okay."

Do you see how they are essentially questions and give the opportunity for the participant to reject the activity? What do you do if they say "no?" Take a moment to discuss, or think about how you would handle that situation.

Giving commands that are clear and have actionable instructions (Billy do a front glide with me) automatically imply that you, the instructor, are in control and should be listened to. When we turn our commands into questions, we give that implied authority back to the participant and give them the option of rejecting our commands. This is a subtle yet powerful erosion of your authority as a swim instructor.

Remember, we are in a potentially fatal environment and we need to make sure that our swimmers are safe. If they are in the habit of doing whatever they want or picking and choosing which commands to follow, then they are more likely to get themselves in a situation where they might hurt themselves or others by not listening to directions.

When you teach swim lessons, you may have five different students who either listen to your commands and those who do not. Often times you can influence all the participants when you give clear expected goals and commands. Ensure that you follow through and enforce your commands to get consistent results.

You can teach effective swim lessons and give clear commands by dropping the word "Okay" from the end of your sentences. Most people that begin teaching swim lessons are unsure of giving commands to children or adults.

New instructors often feel the need to ask if the participants understand the commands or if they heard the instructions.

Typically, the new teachers are looking for some visual or verbal indication that the participant both heard that command and understood it.

They attempt to accomplish this by saying, "Okay," at the end of their sentence when instead they should ask, "Did you hear me," or "Do you understand?"

Here are two exercises you can do on deck during a swim lesson to get out of the "Okay" habit.

Have someone sit on the deck and listen to a swim lesson.

Count the number of times the swim instructor says the word "okay." Attempt to count only the instances where it falls at the end of a sentence. Phrases like, "Okay, we're going to…" are fine and should not be counted.

If you are teaching, remove "okay" from your vocabulary and challenge yourself to use a different work to signify readiness. When you want to ask a question do it completely instead of using assumptive

shorteners.
Example:

Use, "Joey, did you hear me?" Instead of, "Do a front float, okay?"

Use, "Billy, do a front float with me. Do you remember what a front float is?" Instead of, "Billy, let's do a front float together, okay?"

A part of saying "okay" at the end of your sentences and how that turns your command into a questions is the rising inflection, or the rising tone of your voice when you ask, "okay?" When you read the commands, "Billy, we're going to do a front glide, okay?" Read it by giving the command before the "okay" as a strict command, then change the tone of your voice to say "okay" as a question. Most of you will speak in a higher voice to signify the questions. When you do that attached to a command, you effectively turn the whole instruction and command into a question itself when you originally intended to give a command, and then ask a follow-up. Feel free to take the time to communicate well by asking in detail the actual question you want to ask; "did you hear me," "do you understand?" When the word "okay" and the rising tone, or higher voice at the end combine, you get a confusing and unsure command and instructor that will not produce the results that you could be getting. Drop the okay, and keep your voice stable and firm.

Our goal is to be effective communicators and to give clear and easy to follow commands. When we tack on the word "okay" at the end of our sentences we are no longer giving easy to follow commands and instead asking questions that could be ignored. While small instances of saying "okay" is acceptable, you should do your best to avoid saying it and turning your clear commands into questions.

Be curt

- Not Kurt, but brief, quick, and direct. Speak with a period at the end of your sentences.

- Do this. Do that. Do them five times. Ready? Go.

Claim Authority

You are in charge. For the swimmers to be safe, and to learn they need to follow your commands. They'll listen.

Discussion Items:

Form partners and tell your partner to do three things, but at the end of each command add the word "okay."

Partner should always respond with a "no." Do it again without adding "okay." Is it more difficult to ignore the command without the "okay?"

What other questions can "okay" at the end of the sentence really be asking? Example: "Billy, do a front float okay?" 'Okay' might mean are you ready?

Why is giving a clear non-question command important?

Can you use volume or tone to make a command a question?
Hint: rising at the end

Earning Trust

Through repeated honesty.

Through consistency. Through speaking with commands and encouragement.

You may have excellent command language, and you may be exceedingly charismatic (good looking, sweet-talking, wonderful sunny person) but if your students do not trust you they will cling terrified to the walls and benches. Beyond our language and our demeanor, we need to earn the trust of our participants. We can do that by consistently being honest with them.

When we give commands, we should also give clear and appropriate descriptions of how we will help and assist our participants.

Earning trust is the most important and fundamental part of teaching.

To run a fun and effective swim lesson you must earn the trust of your participants. This is true for beginning swim lessons, to level 3 where they're learning to side breathe, and swim teams. All participants in your program need to trust your word and know that you're there to help, not berate or belittle them.

When we earn the participant's trust they'll be more likely to reach for the next skill. They'll respond when we encourage them to put in a little more effort, they'll move without hesitation when you ask them to push off the wall to you across a gap as deep and wide to them as the Grand Canyon. When you've earned their trust, they will perform to their best.

The best way to earn trust is to be honest, be consistent, and to follow slow incremental progressions where they can expect the next step and have multiple opportunities in a caring and loving environment to fail, and improve. Earn your swimmer's trust, and you'll do wonders with them.

Essential actions of honesty to instill trust (steps you can DO to earn trust):

Give swimmers an option to participate. We use command language to get compliance, but if swimmers refuse or cry, we move on and work with the next member of the group.

Do not ignore the "no" student, but do not waste your time on them. Allow them to decline and express disappointment at their decision.

Give excessive praise to those participants that do engage.

Refusing to participate does not mean they get to leave the water or refuse all activities.

Give participants an opportunity to choose whether they go underwater with each activity, and follow through.

Doing jumps? Ask first, "Do you want to go underwater?" Follow through with response and drop the issue. We want those comfortable taking commands and knowing they can trust us. We will get them underwater eventually; do not double down on simple jumps.

Doing supported front glides? Ask during the glide, "Can you put your whole face in the water?" If no response or the terrified stare, amend it to, "Well, if not your whole face how about your chin?"

Remain standing; remain still, planted to the exact location you were when a swimmer does something to you off a bench or into deeper water.

Earn trust by honestly saying, "Push off to me," and DO NOT MOVE.

Remain where you are when they do a front glide to you

unassisted.

Walking backwards as a child struggles to swim or breath is the single worst thing you can possibly do. Absolutely under no circumstance should you run away from a swimmer attempting to swim to you.

Use another more comfortable swimmer to demonstrate a modified activity to demonstrate how it will look. Sometimes seeing someone else do something without putting a face in the water or doing something unwanted will allow them to overcome their fear.

Knowing you will follow through on your promise of doing a modified version of an activity will help earn trust to do more things outside of comfort zones.

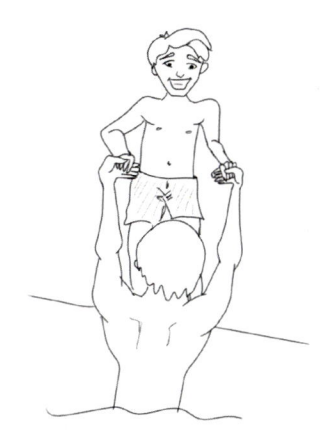

Do what you say

- Give clear instructions to your participants, but also follow through on the words you use.

- If you say you're going to keep them above water, do it.

Don't move.

- Swimming is scary. If a swimmer puts their face down and starts kicking to you DO NOT MOVE! Stay where you are. Build trust by being there to help.

Smile, praise

- The more you smile, the more you praise swimmer's the more they'll like & trust you.

Discussion Items:

What are some other ways you can earn trust through your actions?

Why is trust important to swimming lessons?

Can you be trustworthy if you are forcing someone to go underwater once in a lesson, despite protests of not wanting to?

Can you think of a situation where you should back up while a swimmer attempts to reach you?

Using Images

People don't think in what "not to do."

Create memorable associations with odd connections.

Example: "Like your bedsheets snake-sneaking up stairs for fly k."

How can you use crazy and ridiculous images to get better results to your instructions? Think of a farmer's market stall. Inside that stall is a Weaver that turns thread into cloth, but instead of using colors puts apples, oranges, and strawberries woven with the thread into the loom. People buy the fruit infused cloth and are confused by the lumpy sheets and slowly rotting fruit smell and flurry of fruit flies that show up a few days later. Be like that fruit Weaver that gives instructions and direction woven through with creative exciting and strange images.

We learn better by associating things with images. Our brains are wired to remember the fantastical exciting and different. Hearing the same boring script repeatedly can be effective and provide the direction needed to succeed, but it is better to flavor it with the salt of creativity. Here is an example:

> *We are going to do three x streamline + 3 strokes of freestyle. Focus on keeping your body straight, and looking down.*

> *We're going to do this 3 times: streamline + 3 strokes of freestyle. Try to make your body like a giant mutant carrot with arms to stay straight and near the surface. Pretend your body is an orange carrot shooting through the water.*

Which explanation do you think will have a much more engaged participant? While the first one is exactly correct and an ideal way to give a command, the second one has those same commands and direction but with a fantastical crazy image inserted into it. What you will see if you give these image-laden directions is your participants more engaged because they will be able to visualize what you are asking them to do. Let your mind spurt out image related directions for most of your swimming skills. You can absolutely use the scripts and instructions detailed in section 1 of this training workbook, or from any of the lesson plans. Make them better by salting them with images related to what you are attempting to achieve. Here are a few examples of what fruit laden cloth commands you can give:

- Your feet should be like the leaves on top of a wild carrot pushing it forward. Stay in streamline while you finish your breaststroke kick.
- Do 10 trampoline soldiers with a flip on 5 and 10 (bobs).
- Your goal is to be the arrow we shoot off the wall through the water. Your body should be straight and long immediately when you begin pushing.
- When you swim freestyle, try to remember a right angle, or the corner of a box and you are looking at your elbow to find the last crumb of cake, as your arms recover over the water.
- Paint the water behind you with your toes as you move your legs up and down as if you are waving a paintbrush.
- Do a flip at the wall and let your feet brush the wall as you do your flip. Your goal is to "paint" the wall with your toes as they slide down the wall.
- Every time you kick in breaststroke turn your body into a surfboard and let your kick, push you through the water as you 'ride the glide.'

Use this with beginners when you are being silly and exciting in the middle of an activity. For youngest swimmers we recommend that you give your instructions and commands as clearly and as concise and succinctly as possible without these image laden add ons. Instead with the younger most beginning swimmers, give the instructions clearly, then during the activity use image rich words to describe what you are looking for. Here are a few examples:

- Instructions: "We are going to do front glides with support from me. Remember to look down and kick your feet." Image rich corrections: "Remember to put your mouth in the water to talk to the fishes," "Kick your feet behind you as we do this, you need to really flop your feet like you're trying to untie your shoes but don't have hands!"

- Instructions: "Ok, we are going to kick on the kick-boards from this bench to the next one. Do it 5 times where each way you go counts as 1." Image rich corrections: "Grab the top of the kick-board and keep your arms straight like you're hanging off the side of a cliff." "Stay low on the surface instead of jumping up into the air. You want to be a torpedo that shoots straight through the water instead of bobbing up and down like a buoy."

To give image rich corrections takes a lot of practice and repetition to do well. Do your best to tailor your words to your students or participants taking particular note to use things you know they are familiar with. Fruits, vegetables, and general objects are best as they are more likely recognized by younger participants.

Remember weird.

People associate memories with the fantastical, the strange, and the novel. Be weird and playful. Talk about giant splashing baby seals or play pretend there are birds in the sky.

Image-ination

Imagination creates interesting images.

Connect with swimmers through familiar and strange. Pumpkins that fly cheeseburgers that don't get soggy.

Practice and Fail

Begin with cliches (as wet as water!) and move towards creative. You'll improve the more you practice.

Discussion Items:

What is an image?

Come up with three swimming related images to teach any swim skill.

Think in pictures and then describe the picture. What pictures do you think of that can represent Soldier Position, Back float, and putting your face in the water?

When would you **not** speak in dense image language to a swim class?

Constant Feedback

Talk all of the time. Do all of the voices.
Goal: Targeted feedback to get maximum results.
Goal: Give feedback for every single attempt to every swimmer.

How and when should you give feedback, or commentary about how a swimmer is doing in your classes?

The answer is pretty simple:

Always provide feedback.

Your participants should learn to expect that you will watch and talk to them after every attempt.

If you tell your participants to do something, it is your responsibility, as the instructor, to give feedback on how they did.

Even if you do not see a swimmer, you should acknowledge that you missed their attempt.

Make an effort to watch them on their next attempt and give some sort of feedback.

The whole purpose of swim lessons, beyond the first priority of safety, is to teach swimming.

Give useful feedback.

Our intent is to provide a quality swim lesson where a participant learns something beyond just mentally knowing a thing but to also actually physically to do it.

The most difficult part is teaching someone to change his or her physical behavior and to move in a precise specific motion that is unnatural and at odds with our basic automatic response.

We literally need to teach both how the participant should think, and how they need to master their own body to move in the way we want them to.

Here are some examples of feedback. While reading them think, which ones are useful to the participant and which do nothing to improve the swimmer's ability?

- Well done. Good job.
- Great front float with your face in the water. Next time remember to kick too.
- Good job on your streamline.
- Well done putting your face in the water, but next time attempt to look down instead of forward.
- What was that? You didn't even put your face in on your streamline! Go back and do it again.
- Next time tilt your head back and put your ears in the water, but well done on your back kicks.
- Good.
- Eh, not great.

Which of these examples of "feedback" is effective?

The best examples of feedback are the ones that clearly state what the swimmer did, then give an alternative action on the next attempt.

You did this.

Next time do that.

"You didn't lock your thumb."

"Next time lock your thumb."

It doesn't have to be that basic, but it illustrates the point. You can say something like, we'll your arms didn't come over the water. Next time make sure you reach for the ceiling with every stroke like a wide circle instead of doggy paddling."

Before we get into the nuances of different types of feedback we're going to continue with discussing HOW often you should be giving it.

Ideally, you will provide every swimmer with feedback on something on every single attempt.

That isn't entirely plausible. There are times when you're doing things all at once where you won't be able to do it.

However, giving feedback every single attempt should be the goal, and the standard by which we measure our efforts.

Position yourself in a logical spot to see every round. We recommend you set up your lesson area so that participants can keep moving with short pauses. Looking at this picture you can see how the instructor is outside the bench area. They're close enough to respond if they need to (if a swimmer struggles) but they're planted in one location where they'll speak to every participant as they move through their rotation of skills.

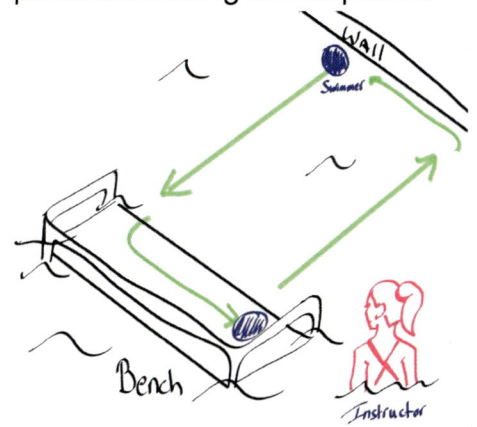

Swimmers in this setup would do something like 6-8 streamlines or glides from the wall to the bench and back again, rotating like a miniature circle swim.

Every time the swimmer gets to the instructor they would receive feedback specific for them.

"Well done on your last streamline. Remember to kick your feet stronger. They were dragging."

If you don't have benches and do something like "one at a time" then give feedback every time the swimmer gets to you, the instructor, and every time they return to the wall. One or two words will suffice.

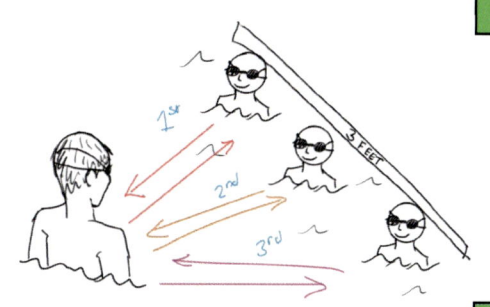

Keep speaking. Keep providing feedback on every attempt.

Maximize Methods

- Leverage your setup so that you can continue to provide feedback.

- Organize your class and system where you get an opportunity to speak and be heard by swimmers.

Avoid chaos

The worst instructors at giving feedback are the ones that are not in control.

Demand compliance. Rule with a benevolent iron fist. Ensure swimmers hear and follow your commands and feedback.

Admit failure

"I'm sorry. I missed it."

Acknowledge it and move on. Watch the next time.

Discussion Items:

Which of the above examples provide no skill changing feedback?

What are some key characteristics of good feedback?

Is number 5 example above something you would ever say in a lesson? When would you? When wouldn't you?

Have someone demonstrate five jumping jacks. Give them 2 pieces of effective good feedback and one ineffective or empty feedback.

63

Praise and Feedback Types

Reward effort.

Allow for failure. Expect it, encourage it, and make another attempt.

Teaching swimming can be challenging, but it is incredibly rewarding and translates to a better life after swim instruction.

If you can master how to give effective feedback using efficient praise types you'll carry communication skills throughout the rest of your life that will serve to your benefit.

We need to change the physical behavior of our participants to learn a very precise and specific way of moving your body to move through the water efficiently and well.

Changing and manipulating body motion can be extremely difficult. We can make our job easier by giving the correct type of praise to see increased results and have swimmers that are more successful.

Above all, Praise the Effort, not the "intelligence" or "talent."

Praise the person's effort in doing something, not their "smarts," "intelligence," or their "talent."

This is a wildly studied concept. Summarizing a number of studies, there was a large sample size of students.

Participants were separated into two groups.

Both groups took the same test of moderate difficulty.

Group 1 was told that they were "very smart" and that is why they did well on their first test.

Group 2 was told that they did well on their test because they "put in a lot of effort and tried very hard."

Both groups were then given a series of tests; one of a very easy level, followed by one extremely difficult and outside their ability range.

The goal was to see how well they did on their initial praise. Finally, they were given a final test that matched the difficulty of the first test.

What researchers found was that students in group 1, the very smart students, did worse on both the difficult test and the final test.

They actually scored lower on the same difficulty test as the first one.

Students in group 2, who were told they put in a lot of effort into their test taking, scored much better than group 1 on both the difficult test and the final similar level test.

What they discovered was that when you're told you are intelligent, you don't put any effort into your work and you expect to do well.

When you fail, you doubt yourself and your ability and feel like an impostor and second guess everything because you failed and are therefore "not intelligent."

Alternately, if you are praised for your hard work and effort you ascribe your success to your actions: studying, attention, time dedication, etc. When you are met with difficulties you react by putting in more energy to success and actually do better as a result.

For our purposes in swimming lessons, we want to quickly and effectively produce the best results when we are teaching swim lessons. Your goal should be to praise the effort or the attempt at doing something.

When you give feedback to your students, swimmers, or participants remember to praise and reward the effort and the attempt at something new instead of saying things like, "you are so talented," "you're so smart!"

Examples of effort worthy praise:

"Well done putting your face in the water, I can tell you really made a good attempt!"

"Congratulations on doing that front float alone! We've worked so much on it. That effort has paid off!"

"Well done on your streamline. Great job locking your thumb, next time attempt to squeeze your ears too. I know you can do it."

Finally, here are some examples from three of the studies about how to give positive effort praise:

• Praise your child for her strategies (e.g., "You found a really good way to do it")

• Praise your child for specific work (e.g., "You did a great job with those math problems")

• Praise your child for his persistence or effort (e.g., "I can see you've been practicing" and "Your hard work has really paid off")

Praising kids for effort (and not innate ability) may help them develop a better mindset for learning. For more information, see "Harmful beliefs: How a theory of intelligence can hamper your child's ability to learn."

Praise Effort

- Great attempt! I can see how you're working at getting better!
- Yes! That time was awesome. Do more of that!
- That was the best attempt!

Use nonverbals

- Smile.
- Give a "thumbs up"
- Don't be afraid of saying, "no. That wasn't good" as long as you also reward positive behavior

Can you say "Fail?"

- YES! Use the word without negativity and associate it with not accomplishing a task.

Discussion Items:

Give 3 examples of "intelligence" praise for doing front crawl with breathing well.

Give 3 examples of "effort" praise for doing breaststroke well.

Is "I'm glad you attempted that back float." Effective praise? Does it satisfy the "praise the effort?"

Do you think praising intelligence creates laziness later on? Why or why not?

Replace bad habits with new, better alternatives.

You did this, next time do that.

In addition to knowing to praise effort over innate ability we need to discuss how to correct someone's bad behavior.

Not like splashing other children in the face or biting toys.

How do we get someone that lifts their head up when they swim to instead look down?

How do we change their physical behavior while they swim? What do we say, what do we do to get them to change what they're doing?

Do you think that saying, "Don't lift your head up" works?

What do you think about when someone shouts, "Don't spill my water!?"

I'll bet you start repeating in your head, "spill the water, spill the water…"

People don't hear the word "don't" they instead hear the verbs of shouted negatives.

"Don't lift your head up" turns into "lift your head up."

If we change our feedback to match and account for this fact we'll get better results quicker.

Closely tied to giving effort based praise and feedback, we want to look at negative corrections and positive corrections.

For beginners we have a clean slate of swimming; a blank canvass to work with. As we progress, our participants will start to develop habits that either are in line with our swimming technique goals or fall outside that narrow range of movement.

One great example is lifting the head up when doing a streamline and then front glide and front crawl. Most beginner swimmers want to see where they are going and like to lift their forehead up so they can see the direction that they are moving. Unfortunately, this creates a bad habit and makes swimming more difficult. When the head rises the body needs to balance like a seesaw and the feet begin to sink. When the feet sink, the body then is dragged down and the head will eventually sink too.

You will remember from section 1 that we are looking for a long body-line and a straight body like soldier position to swim well. Part of that is looking down. When we see someone lift his or her head up should we give feedback that focuses on the negative or offers an alternative action to address the negative?

Discuss the merits of each item of feedback:

"Don't look up Johnny! Go again, ready go."

"Johnny, when you do your streamline remember to look down at the bottom with your whole face."

"No, don't do that! Stop lifting your head up when you breathe."

"I want you to look down while you're breathing. Attempt to do that as much as possible, ideally the whole time."

Research shows that when you, as a teacher, focus on negatives the participants do not learn as much or change their behavior.

They may conceptually know what they should be doing, but their internal voice will be saying what not to do instead of repeating what they should do. One of my favorite examples is this.

Do this activity:
Water, and 1 glass or cup

Fill glass or cup to the top with water. Participants should walk at least 10-20 feet with the full to the brim cup of water. While walking repeat aloud, "don't drop a drop, don't spill the water, don't spill the water, and don't spill the water."

Fill the cup again to the top, and walk the same distance, but repeat to yourself, "I will walk slowly and carefully barely moving the cup."

The theory suggests that your brain will ignore the negative qualifier, "don't" and just hear, "spill the water, spill the water, spill the water." That internal command will make you more likely to spill the water. When you say what you will do instead "walk slowly and carefully and barely moving the cup," you will be more likely to NOT spill any water because you are telling yourself over and over things you will do well.

When you give feedback that is strictly negative, the participants will only hear the incorrect command, and it will make it more difficult to achieve success doing what you want them to do. Instead, offer an alternative action or command to modify their incorrect behavior or skill. They will hear your voice giving them a successful option, and they can repeat that.

"Look down, look down, look at the floor" is a much better monologue than, "Whoops, looked forward, look down. Oh no, I am looking forward again, don't do that, look up? Sideways?"

You did this...
Clearly state what the person did on their most recent attempt:

"You didn't kick last time."

"On the last 25 you took three breaths lifting your head up."

Next time do...
Provide an alternative action that the swimmer can aim towards, or do instead of their bad behavior.
"Next time, only turn your head to the side keeping your cheek laying on the water like a pillow."

Fail. Here's why:
If a swimmer fails a challenge or an activity tell them why. Give them clear examples and strategies to succeed.

Discussion Items:

Watch someone walk across the front of the room in streamline but not doing one of the three things: a) lock thumb, b) squeeze ears, c) looking down (straight ahead while walking).

Correct their action using negative language. Then, correct their action using alternative success language.

Do you think you can never use negative language?

What are some examples of positive alternative language feedback for someone who does not glide between the kick on breaststroke and the next arm stroke?

Feedback Layer Cake

State what they did, give alternate action, give a positive.

Remain caring, positive, and encouraging.

You have done a good job so far paying attention to this training and going through each of the discussion items. As we continue the course, remember to pay particular attention to the reasons behind the discussion items. Are they written in a way to guide discussion? Or are they random fact regurgitating questions?

In a broad sense, that paragraph immediately before was a feedback layer cake. I positively praised your effort in taking the training seriously, whether you are or not, and then gave you a correction, or focus to improve upon as you continue going forward. This is a great general template to give feedback. Here are a few ways to describe giving feedback:

"You did [whatever the participant did], Next time do [explain how to improve]."

State what they did, then explain how to do correctly

Demonstrate their action.

Demonstrate the correction

Point out a positive, follow with a related correction

Our general goal is to speak a positive, or a statement of what they did objectively (without anger or judgment), and follow that with a correction or an alternative route to skill success.

"You did this; next time do it like this."

If you are working on streamlines, you can say to the participants, "Well done looking down, but you didn't squeeze your ears. Next time remember to and look down."

That statement covers what they did well, states what they did, and encourages a future change: squeeze your ears.

Combine this with constantly giving feedback, praising the effort, and replacing bad habits with new alternative actions.

You get this simple formula:

State what the participant did: something they did well, or something glaringly wrong objectively (statement of fact without negative tone or emotion attached).

Provide correction:

If you praised something, they did well, and then give correction on skill related to current activity. Example: doing streamlines and you praised them looking down.

Next time participant should kick the whole time.

If you corrected a wrong attempt, then give clear description on how to succeed.

Example: doing streamlines and participant looked up or forward the whole time.

Next time, remember to look down while you streamline the whole time.

Thumbs up as a currency:

You do not always have to speak after every attempt.

You can use body language, signs and gestures to convey praise or disapproval.

As a swim coach on a loud and difficult to hear pool deck, I do not always shout corrections or praises. Sometimes I just give a thumbs up, or two thumbs up, and if someone had a particularly notable improvement, I will clap and cheer.

Likewise, you can make small gestures of disapproval when both participant and instructor know exactly what the participant needs to correct.

You can frown, or shake your head "no" to signify the need for correction. Sometimes these basic and small gestures are more effective than stopping and talking to the participant. When we do 3 x streamline + 3 strokes of Free + a flip, the swimmers I work with are conditioned to look at me after each of their attempts.

Usually I have 6-12 participants in my small group with three going at the same time.

If I see, the participant in it looks mostly good, I will give a thumbs up directed at the participant, or if I have missed the attempt, I will apologize and say I missed it. Where there is a need for more correction, I will follow the 1 positive, 1 correction formula: "You did this well, or you did this, next time do this."

Because of doing these feedbacks and sometimes non-verbal feedback, the swimmers I work with are conditioned to looking at me on deck after each of their attempts.

When I give a thumbs up, I often see them celebrate in some small way; a muted "yes" to themselves, or a fist pull in happiness.

The thumbs up is a sign of approval and success.
Use it.

Overall positivity
- You can skip the last positive statement if you need to, or if you feel your feedback doesn't need it.
- Overall, you should convey a sense of positivity to all swimmers.

Nurturing, caring
- Your swimmers should feel like you care about them. They should trust that you want what is best.
- Use language to lift up their spirits, create smiles, and earn their respect.

You failed!
- Avoid taking pleasure out of other people's failures.
- Build up, not destroy.

Discussion Items:

Are there any other ways to give praise outside of the one positive, 1 corrective formula?

Can you elaborate on corrections or positives beyond just one? What if a participant did so many things that were so obvious and entirely bad, you need to correct everything?

Is there a need to address every mistake each attempt?

Does stating their action that was wrong violate the positive praise expectation?

Total Active Engagement

Keep the most people doing something as possible in a safe, manageable way.

Leverage frameworks, habits, benches.

With Total Active Engagement, we want everyone to be active at the same time simultaneously attempting to accomplish a task.

Think of this as everyone moving at the same time with a common purpose. This can be a challenging thing to accomplish. Our goal should be to involve as many participants as we can at once, but we need to balance the "time on task" mandate with providing a safe lesson.

Total Active Engagement are games, songs, or activities you have everyone do at the same time. A few examples are:

- Bake a Cake
- Kicking with barbells or kick-boards (to participants that can use them safely in water deeper than they can stand)
- Glides from a bench to a bench, or point A to point B and back.
- Walking through hula hoops, moving in a circle (different "tolls" as you pass through hoop each time; chin in water, nose under, eyes in, etc.)
- Kicking while sitting on the side of the pool
- 3x streamline + 5 strokes FREE + 1 breath to the side + flip

You can see from the list above that most of the activities are basic. When we get to better quality swimmers, we can introduce activities that are more complex and attempt to maximize how many are participating at the same time.

From a swim lesson perspective where you are teaching beginners, we can easily utilize Total Active Engagement when we have a zero depth pool, or a shallow enough pool where everyone can walk on their own feet alone. The shallow water allows movement and provides a safer environment for the swimmers to attempt activities.

If we do not have that shallow water, how can we maximize our participant's time and still provide a safe lesson? We should do our best to modify our activities to include more than one participant at a time, and push the edge of effective and engaging.

Imagine a scenario where we have five swim participants about 3 or 4 years old. Some of them will go underwater on their own, and some will not. We have a three and ½-foot pool with platforms that can be wobbly.

Participants stand on the platforms and their chest remains above the water. They can walk around, but the space is not very large. How can we maximize their motion and action in the water, but still provide a safe lesson? We want to accomplish the following goals: Go Underwater, do front glides with support (they do not go under on their own, and water is too deep for alligator walks), do back glides with support.

Break down the skill to its simplest parts in an effort to make it easier for everyone to do.

For example, going underwater:

Total Active Engagement:

"Everyone we're going to do this together. Put you chin in the water and say my name! Now, we're going to do it again, but this time put your lips in the water and say YOUR name, and let there be bubbles!"

Consider using swimming aides to help your students stay above water, but work on the horizontal body position.

Give them a barbell or a noodle to put under their arms. The swimmers can then move from a certain point on the bench to another, or if there is not enough room for that, they can go from the bench to the instructor and back.

The best option would be multiple times from bench A to bench B as long as the instructor was there supervising and watching the whole time.

With a class of five, we would recommend only having two swimmers participate at a time with floating assists in case one falls off.

The remaining members of the class would remain on the bench.

This leads us nicely into the next option.

Instead of doing Total Active Engagement do Some Active Engagement.

If you cannot safely get everyone participating in the activity at the same time, then reduce the number that actively participating.

Let others wait.

Have two or three people moving while the other two or three wait.

This way you get more people involved, reduce the amount of downtime, but accommodate for safety concerns.

Give commands
- Expect swimmers to do what you announce you're doing as a group.
- Encourage everyone to participate.
- Do it yourself too!

Use the familiar
- Keep your swimmers moving. Have them go from bench to bench in the same counter-clockwise motion.
- Start with walking, build up to swimming.

Change the details
- Same challenges or activities with minor variations are a great way to keep interest going.

Discussion Items:

Describe an effective use of Total Active Engagement for a level 1 class (pick an activity and explain how you would get everyone in a class engaged at the same time at your pool).

Is there a scenario or time that you would NOT do something all at once?

Why do we want everyone doing something at the same time?

What are some ways you can modify Total Active Engagement to address safety concerns or swimmer limitation?

One on One

Not the best choice, but useful in challenging circumstances.

Effective with smaller groups.

Perhaps the exact opposite of Total Active Engagements, where everyone is moving at the same time, are One on One activities.

Here, the instructor and the participant work in a one on one setting where the other members of the class are waiting for their turn in a safe location, a bench, or in a specific area in the pool. Participants then take turns engaging with the teacher.

Typically this is specific to tasks outside the swimmer's ability to do on their own and requires direct swim instructor involvement.

The swim instructor may need to physically support the swimmer when doing front glides if the swimmer is not comfortable yet putting their face in the water, or not comfortable doing it in water they cannot stand in.

Here are a few examples of when you should use One on One instruction:

- Working on going underwater together: chin, lips, nose, eyes, whole head
- When doing front glides with beginners that do not put their face in the water, or if they do lift their head up looking forward
- When doing back floats and glides with beginners, or intermediate swimmers
- When teaching a new skill like front crawl arms
- When doing jumps from the side with a participant that does not go underwater or cannot swim, but will go underwater
- When diving for rings with swimmers that cannot get all the way down alone
- Many, many others

One on One instruction can be extremely effective but it comes at the cost of wasted time for the other participants in the class.

The swim instructor is working with only 1 person while the other 4 participants are sitting around doing nothing. A good instructor will give swimmers a dynamic and interesting task to accomplish while they wait.

This is INCREDIBLY difficult to do every time well and if you have a suggestion for this, PLEASE speak up now.

Most new swim instructors immediately go to, "practice your arm circles while you wait!"

That is typically a good thing to do as it is safe, it works on a great learned skill with a specific motion, and it could take a lot of time.

However, it is really boring to actually do over and over, and eventually the young participants will get tired moving their arms in an unfamiliar motion (especially over the head) and stop doing it after 10-20 seconds.

You will see some very dedicated participants that do it endlessly but they are extremely rare and will likely progress out of that class quickly.

Examples of activities to do while waiting:

- Dive for rings
- Walk through a hula hoop
- Do 10 lazy puppets that turn into soldier position
- Do 10 Reach for the stars and then reach for your toes
- Do two direction arm circles; one arm goes forward other goes back, then switch

I encourage you to let your swimmers explore the water on their own if it is safe to do so.

If your program uses benches or platforms that your youngest swimmers can stand on then let them play. Let them go underwater on their own.

Let them practice gliding back and forth while getting submerged objects or throwing splash toys. Play and self guidance is a great way to discover a feel for the water.

Sometimes I hear lifeguards and pool managers scold kids for going underwater when it isn't their turn. Does that make sense?

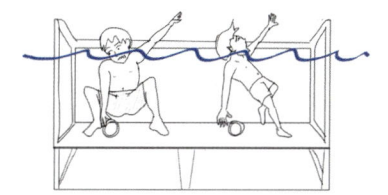

Aren't we trying to get them to go underwater frequently?

Let your group play, if it is safe.

If they are hanging onto the side shivering in water too deep for them to touch, reevaluate your location and see if you can get somewhere they can stand.

Let them play

- Take every effort possible to let your swimmers play or do something productive while they wait.
- Avoid giving boring tasks like arm circles. They won't do them.

Be quick. Talk fast

- We want to maximize the amount of time each swimmer does something.
- Get through turns quickly. Give commands, support when needed, and send them back to the bench.

Relocate

- Maximize the space in your pool by getting benches or platforms. Shallow water is best.

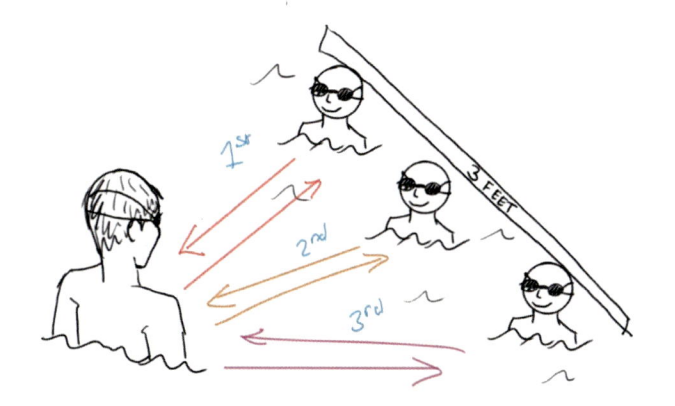

Discussion Items:

What are some benefits of One on One instruction? Negatives?

What is the opposite of One on One instruction?

Can you think of some great ways to keep the swimmers who are waiting engaged and doing something swimming specific?

List out some skills that are better done One on One, as opposed to doing in a wave, or a group, or all together.

Rotation Method

Like driving a car; same flow of traffic.

Keep moving. Rotate through and queue up along wall or on benches.

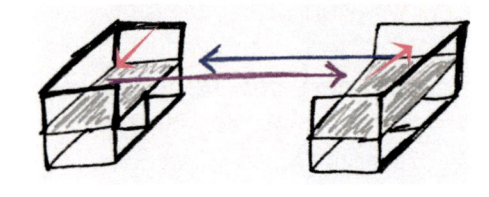

The rotation method is ideal for when you have a large class and a facility that does not allow for waves, or total active engagement.

Instead, when the activity or the pool demands, we need to work with swimmers on a one on one basis.

We can speed up that slow One on One process with the rotation method. Here is a quick graphic that basically illustrates the general flow.

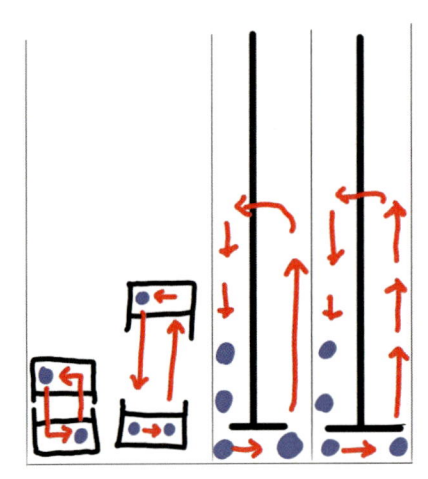

The swimmer, or student, goes to the instructor, and then returns to the bench or wall to wait in line until their turn comes up again.

Swimmers move in a general rotation where they will always begin at a certain location, go to the instructor (either with or without help) and then will return to the starting location at the end of the line.

This is generally on the other side of the group from where they began. If you are using a lane in a swim pool look at the graphic above and to the right. The swim instructor would be standing near the curved arrow arching left. There they would provide feedback, and return them to the line to wait and take their next turn.

One of the biggest benefits of the rotation method is that it can be standardized.

When every teacher utilizes it in the program, every student knows right away what the format will be where they start doing a skill or activity.

There will be no confusion on where the swimmer needs to go, or what to do when they get there.

We should generally attempt to use the rotation method for every activity that requires instructor assistance (mostly levels 1 - 2).

Here are some activity examples that should use the rotation method:

- Supported Front glides
- Supported back glides
- Unsupported front glides a short distance (1/2 body length or 1 body length)
- Unsupported back glides a short distance 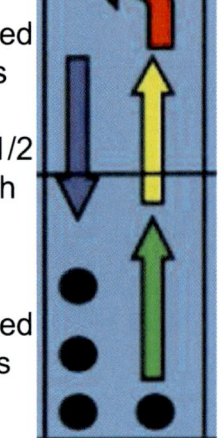
- Unsupported front glides that transition to supported front crawl arm practice
- Kicking with a kick-board or barbell for beginners
- Jumps from the side with the instructor

In each example the participant would either go with the instructor from the starting location, or would briefly move to the instructor unsupported and then be supported. Whenever the participant encounters the swim instructor the teacher should give feedback relevant to the activity, and then return the participant back to the class area. They can do this by launching them forward in streamline (arms forward, head down, push off my knee), or by walking the participant back to the class area and getting them to safety.

If possible, the best option is to send the participant back to the class location unassisted where they do the same activity back focusing on the feedback you just gave them when they got to you.

Further variation is putting two benches together and going from Bench to Bench using the same rotation method.

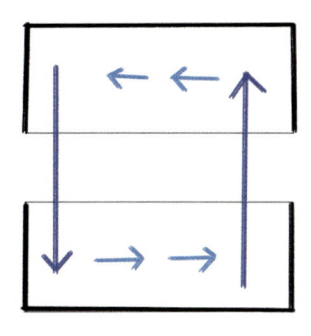

We can even use this rotation method when we have one bench and kids that can stand in water next to the wall but not further out. Place a bench at about the flags, or 5 yards away, and aim it at the wall.

Experiment with your pool and your unique situation to keep your swimmers moving as quickly as possible. How can you keep them "rotating through" your activities to maximize action, movement, and attention?

Keep moving!
- Avoid making your swimmers wait for you to say "go."
- Set up systems where swimmers know to do things 4, 5, or 6 times without stopping.

Circle swimming
- Lap swimmers keep moving. They go down one side and return on the other.
- Take this same concept and shorten the distance.

Move over, and go
- Train the swimmers that they should go once the way is clear. Take your turn, get out of the way.

Discussion Items:

What are some benefits of the rotation method?

Is it okay to not give feedback when a participant returns to the class location, or starting location?

Can two participants go to the instructor at the same time? Can you think of a safe way to accomplish this?

Describe a few other ways you can get swimmers to do something to the instructor and then back to the start location, and make sure everyone gets a turn.

Waves

Send them all at the same time.

Ensure no overlap so swimmers don't swim on top of each other.

Waves are effective at maximizing participation for skills that don't require direct instructor involvement.

Having your participants do activities in a wave like fashion gets more people doing something at the same time than doing something one by one.

One of major challenges of swimming lessons is getting your participants moving and not just sitting on the edge of the pool or standing on the bench doing nothing.

The parents are looking at their children wondering why they're paying for every minute their child sits there doing nothing.

It is a good idea to do 'waves' with any size group, and the ultimate goal is to get as many people doing your activity as possible, safely.

We usually do one on one when the instructor needs to physically support the swimmer at the surface because they cannot touch the bottom or they will not put their face in the water.

Use waves when you can do an activity where you do not need to physically support the participant.

Here are a few activities you can do without support to utilize the "waves" method:

- Kicking on barbell, floaties, or kick-boards. Ideally the participants should be in water they can touch the bottom in, but if not, instructor should be immediately nearby.
- Swimming or streamlining short distances from one spot that the participant can touch the bottom to another place they can touch the bottom.
- Walking from point A to point B
- Generally moving in any area that the participants can stand up with their head above the water on their own.

Attempt to use 'waves' to engage as many people as possible with each activity. If you can safely have more than one person moving at the same time, you should.

Waves are generally a great way to get more than one person moving, but not everyone, so participants can have enough room to move around, and the instructor can easily step in if they need to support anyone.

Consider what would happen if you sent a group of new swimmers that couldn't touch the bottom to you all at the same time.

Would you be able to pick them all up without letting any of them sink underwater?

Would you want 5 level 1 swimmers (who don't go underwater) doing kicks on kick-boards out to water over their head all at the same time?

The answer is, obviously, no.

You should not use waves in every situation.

Use it when you can effectively manage the risk and ensure the safety of your participants.

When you're in water so shallow that everyone can stand like a zero-depth pool, or a beach, then waves is an EXCELLENT tool to do most activities.

76

Waves, all at once

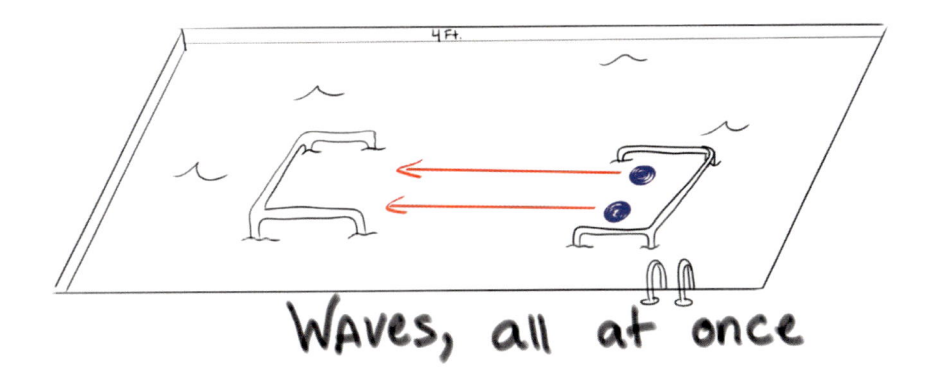

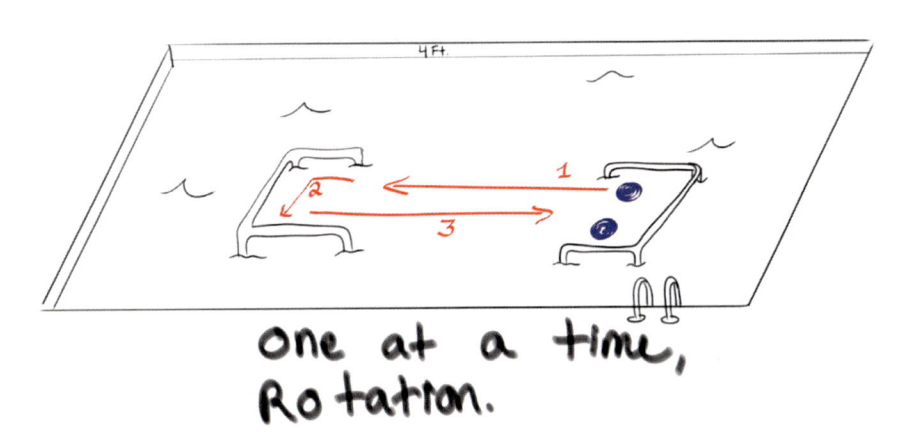

One at a time, Rotation.

Everyone goes!
- Waves have multiple people go at the same time.
- Usually reserved for more advanced groups and levels.

Safety!
- Consider if the situation you're asking your swimmers to do is safe.
- If doing a wave activity make sure that wherever the swimmer goes to they can touch the bottom.

Rotation or Wave?
- Sometimes its easier to do rotation style with swimmers. It manages risk and keeps them moving.

Discussion Items:

When is it safe to use the 'waves' method to have participants do an activity?

Why do we want to use 'waves' over one on one instruction?

Would you do Jumps from the side with a group of kids that don't go underwater in waves? Would you do jumps from the side in waves with a group of swimmers that can swim unassisted?

Describe how using 'waves' in your lesson would increase the "time on task" for each participant?

Maximizing Action

Leverage lesson plans, either those you create or those prescribed by your program.
Go to training.

Most swim lessons are about 30 minutes long. In that time, we have up to 5 participants and one instructor. If divided evenly, that is 6 minutes of one on one instructor to participant time (30 / 5 = 6). Beyond that we have potential distractions like crying children, cold water, clouds, or helicopter parents that hover over the edge of the pool.

A huge challenge for swim instructors is to make sure we are giving as much attention and practice opportunities to each student for as long as possible.

We want to increase that time for each participant to get feedback and interaction with the instructor. We can achieve that goal by maximizing the actions we take during our lessons.

Maximizing action is a combination of making sure everyone is participating and making our activities purposeful. For the general high school or beginner swim instructor, this is not always at the top of their minds.

Most swim instructors are not delving deep into the whys and hows of effective communication and instruction. They likely aren't looking at what a particular swim skill task or teaching technique will best engage the most people in the group and move the class forward in ability. Heck, most veteran swim instructors are not thinking along those lines. Swim lessons just doesn't rank that high on the importance and seriousness scale for most people.

How do you get the most people in your class actively participating?

Is what you are doing moving the class forward by teaching relevant ability level skills?

Maximizing action, is directly addressing these two main points. We can approach this challenge, "maximizing action," from two angles to help swim instructors that are not directly considering this.

#1 We can give swim lesson plans

You can follow the swim lesson plans for each level you're teaching and you'll do a series of skills and activities that are designed to maximize the time spent in the water.

With a swim lesson plan in your hand, you don't need to think about "is this skill or activity bringing my class along the best possible progression to maximize their learning?"

Nope, you have that info right in your hand and you can reference it immediately during a lesson so you don't even need to think about it.

#2 We can do regular swim lesson training

We can better see the larger picture of why we're doing bobs and soldier positions every day when we know that body line and balance ties in to holding a strong core when turning the head and hips to the side to breathe.

When we attend regular training on how to teach swim lessons better we build up our teaching toolbox.

We gain the understanding why each skill is done and for what reason.

Same is true with swim instructors. If you participate by showing up at regular trainings, you'll become a better teacher because your knowledge bank about swimming will increase. Swim instructors that have a

To truly "maximize actions" during a swim lesson is to balance between effectively planning out what skills and activities you're going to do in what specific order, and how are you going to involve the most people at the same time to make the most of the little class time you have.

We can help you get there by giving you swim lesson plans and by increasing your swimming knowledge through regular trainings.

This gives you the tools you'll need to consider all the options you have available and piece together using your own best judgment what will work for this specific group you have today.

People are variables that change dramatically from one moment to the next and we can't always count on a well thought lesson plan or a set script for every action.

Sometimes we need to call an audible, adjust immediately to accommodate specific participant or group needs.

Remember when you make changes to consider if you are doing something that will work on a swim skill, and if it has a purpose.

Look at why you're doing something. Is it to fill time and move the clock quickly so you can get in the hot tub?

Choose activities that build or aim at a specific swimming skill. Do something that makes your swimmers better.

Have a purpose
- Do something for a reason. Want to do kicking? Sure, but why? Do your swimmers have weak kicks? Slow legs?
- Be deliberate with your choices.

Time killers
- Avoid wasting time with repetitive games and boring activities.
- Engage your brain, be creative, do something fun!
- Be entertaining!

Stick to the script
- Standard language makes teaching easier for everyone. Use the same words to be more effective.

Discussion Items:

What are the two main components to maximizing action in a swimming lesson?

Do you think it is important to have a huge depth of swimming knowledge to teach an effective swim class? Are there any tools to help teachers?

Are you supposed to read right off the swim lesson plans during a lesson?

Plan out a 30-minute lesson plan. What does it look like? What are you going to do? Break down each activity into how long it will likely take.

Time on Task

How many minutes during a lesson are your swimmers actively doing something?

How much of your time do they get?

Participants in your swim lessons will want to be actively doing something. Their parents and them are there to learn how to swim, and you have control over that goal. Your actions dictate how well they achieve that goal and how quickly they will progress.

Swimming lesson coordinators track how often participants are actually doing something in their lessons. We want to know how much time is a participant either talking to the instructor, or moving with purpose.

Think of this as good quality review. We ask two questions:

Are the instructors talking to their participants with relevant feedback?

Are they keeping the participants moving?

Someone will sit with a stopwatch and watch a swim lesson.

They will look at one child and start the watch when that child does something at the direction of the instructor.

When the instructor stops talking to them, or they complete their task, the person will stop the watch. At the end of the lesson they will look at the total time that child received attention or direction.

Without reading ahead, how much time does an average participant get in a 30-minute swim lesson? Assume 5 swimmers in a class.

Most swimming lesson participants get 6 minutes of feedback, instruction, and attempts.

The average participant only does something for 6 minutes! Yikes! That is virtually nothing!

6 minutes per person in a 3o minute class is bad.

That means that for 24 minutes of the class the swimmer is doing nothing. Swimming Ideas' goal is to provide swim instructors an easy way to keep their students moving and receiving feedback. We have designed the swim lesson plans to maximize engagement.

Lesson participants should be moving often and be receiving lots of specific feedback.

The previous sections are all designed to increase your participant's "Time on Task." We want you to make sure your class is doing something with a purpose and receiving feedback.

Each swimmer should get at least 20 minutes of activity during a 30-minute lesson. We can achieve this by doing the rotation method without the instructor involved. Swimmers can go from bench to bench, or from place A to place B.

For beginners, you can do waves, or group activities where everyone can stand.

As you get more competent swimmers, you can have more people doing something at the same time. Move away from having 1 person moving at a time, and give as many opportunities to do something.

For example, "Do 5 x streamline from the wall to the bench. Each time you go from one to the other counts as one.

Remember to look down, squeeze your ears, and lock your thumb." The instructor can then spend most of their time correcting those small technique mistakes, and let the swimmers move on their own.

If you must do One on One instruction, attempt to move quickly and cut the amount of time you spend talking.

Give targeted specific feedback, and follow up immediately. Avoid waiting for a response.

Give commands and specific changes using as few words as possible. Swimmers will respond or not and will quickly get another chance to do it again.

For example, "Good job reaching to me, but next time remember to look down." After attempting again, "Good kicks, look down the whole time though."

When doing a One on One rotation, move quickly, give targeted commands, and keep everyone moving.

Avoid being a traffic cop with the whistle and the bright colored vest waving a stop sign around.

Instead, be the coach that gives commentary from the side. Target actual effort and attention to skill work instead of directing traffic flow.

New swim instructors get caught up waving cars while they whistle instead of giving feedback on the quality of driving like a coach or instructor should.

Establish routine, always moving and constant rotations, then ignore it. Give your swimmers clear expectations.

"Do 6 rounds of this without stopping."

Stand nearby and talk about how well they did what you've asked.

Do something
- Make every attempt to engage your swimmers in some fashion.
- Give high fives, say their name as often as possible and do things that require group effort or attention.

Keep talking
- Fill your lessons with the sound of your voice. Be dynamic and entertaining, interesting and captivating things you say and do. Engage them all by speaking loud and a lot.

Wasted time
- Before you do an activity ask yourself, "Will my swimmers be standing around waiting a lot?

Discussion Items:

What are two tactics you can do to make sure swimmers are actively participating?

Who is responsible for increasing each participant's time on task?

Can you think of why 6 minutes per person is the average? What are those instructors doing with the other 24 minutes?

What language can you use to maximize movement while reducing the need to "direct traffic?"

Is there a time and a place to be the traffic cop?

Lesson Plan Organization

Who are you teaching?

Consider progressions and flow, next incremental steps.

Think about the essential swim skills from the beginning of the book. Each item described there can be a skill you can insert into your swim lesson plan.

For example, you can take supported front glides with hands on shoulders and do that first. Immediately after, you can work on going underwater with a game.

Then do supported front glides with hand in hands, while encouraging participants to put their face in the water. Mix and match different level specific skills while remembering the three points above. You can then produce quick swim lesson plans and test them out. If a certain progression does not work, substitute a different skill.

This training workbook gives you all the resources you need: 15 essential swim skills, how to get a class to do each one, and in depth guides on how to teach well.

Consider your class:

You should remember who you are teaching when you create your swim lesson plan. You can ask yourself some simple questions to determine your class makeup.

1. What level are the swimmers?
2. How old are they?
3. What is your goal for this class?

Let us look at #1 first; what level are the swimmers.

Swimming Ideas uses levels to separate out swimmers into relative ability groups.

We call swimmers that cannot go underwater on their own "level 1."

If you are familiar with the different levels, you can define a lot of important information.

Then, you can narrow down your choices when you begin selecting skills to work on in your swim lesson plan.

Define the group's level you want to create a lesson plan for. Next, look at that level's specific ability goals and write your lesson plan with those same goals.

The second question to ask yourself, "how old are your swimmers," will tell you how complex you be.

Younger swimmers need simpler instructions and have shorter attention spans.

With older, or adult swimmers you can be more elaborate if you need to be.

Knowing how old your swimmers are can help shape your skill and game choices. "Buckethead" is an excellent game for beginners, but not ideal for people over 10.

For older swimmers you can tailor your games as "challenges." Make your challenges just at or slightly above your swimmer's ability comfort.

When you know your participant's age, you can craft better lessons. You will be able to create activities that are simple for young swimmers and more complex for older ones.

The third question, "What is your goal for the class," will give you a guide to begin with.

Sometimes your goal will match the level goals.

For example, level one's goal is to go underwater.

Your class day lesson plan could be only about going underwater. You could mix and match many different 'going underwater' activities and games into one lesson.

Maybe your goal is to hit every key skill in level one instead.

When you craft your lesson with this goal, you would do a little bit of front glide, back glide, and going underwater.

A good rule of thumb is to match your goal to the level criteria. Level one: go underwater on own, do front glide with support and face in the water, and do back glide with support with ears in the water.

Think about location; where in the pool will your class be conducted?

Not every class is taught in the same space. Sometimes you'll have a limited area to teach, others you'll have a wide open pool free from distractions and other activities.

There are programs that only teach swim lessons during certain times. The pool will be closed to the general public, and groups of swimmers and teachers will use the space. Many of the outdoor seasonal pools will do this in the morning for camps and group lessons.

Other facilities will have other activities going on in the pool at the same time as your lessons. Maybe there is lap swim so you're limited on which lanes, if any, you can use. Maybe there is an aqua aerobics class with music, or a swim team. There are multiple activities and programs that can happen in a pool during your swim lessons.

When you're considering what you are going to do in your lesson, remember to think about your space. What part of the pool will you have available to teach? Are you able to move around, go to the deep end, or have enough space to work on streamlines? If you are in one small section of the pool you won't be able to do full lengths or longer swims. How will that change your plans?

If you have a small space, do you have any tools like benches, platforms, or floats that swimmers can stand or wait on? Will you be in the deep end? Will the water be over the swimmer's heads? How will they wait for you?

Where you are teaching swimming lessons is just as important a factor as who you're teaching when you're creating a lesson plan.

What to include:

Make your titles and instructions as easy to read as possible.
We recommend writing 3 x SL + 3 FR + Flip because it is a single line, and it denotes a specific flow of actions with shorthand.
"Everyone goes three times, streamline first, then do three strokes of freestyle with kicking, and finish with a flip."
Our standard number of attempts with feedback is 3, but you can change it to 4 or 5. This is something you can change when you're in the lesson. Sometimes the swimmer's attentions are not on task and you need to do fewer, or sometimes they're doing so well you can let them do 5 times.

Best recommendation is to follow this formula, following the sample lesson plans included in the back of the book:

Activity 1, Activity 2 (related to activity 1), Challenge.
Example:
Glides, glides with arm strokes, Do 1 front flip.

Progressions and Flow

Link together like skills; glides with kicks.

Have a target, where do you want to go?

We could write a book solely about "progressions and flow" in your swimming lessons. When you are creating your own lesson plan remember to take small steps. The best point we can distill for you is to teach each skill in small steps.
Begin with a simple skill and add a small more difficult one on top of it. For example: basic simple skill putting your lips in the water. The next step is putting your nose in the water too. The end goal is to go completely underwater, but we are moving towards it in small incremental steps. The closer you make your steps in relation to the easy skill the easier it is to accomplish. Pretend we have a swimmer that does not go underwater on their own. They will not put anything over their eyes underwater.
A good incremental gradual progression would be to start with the chin, then the lips, then the nose. Each step is close to the one before it and we started with the most basic skill: chin in the water.
Let us pretend we have the same swimmer that does not go underwater on their own. This time we start with putting your whole head underwater. The swimmer refuses. If we persist and demand they go underwater with their whole head, we will encounter resistance. The swimmer might lash out or cry and disrupt the lesson. Our goal is to approach new or challenging skills in small incremental steps. In this case, we jumped ahead, beyond, this swimmer's ability comfort level. We know that the swimmer does not go underwater on their own, and our goal is for them to. We cannot only say, "Go underwater" and expect them to do it. Instead, the best choice is to go through the whole incremental underwater progression.
Remember to approach each of your goals from simple to more complex. If our goal is to swim front crawl for 5 meters with breathing, we would begin with streamlines. Front glides, or streamlines, are the first step in teaching front crawl. We can then layer up more difficult items to get to our desired goal. After streamlines we can add kicking, then looking down the whole time. Next we can add arm strokes with kick and in streamline. Finally we can have the swimmers take 1 breath to the side. Each item we add to the basic skill of streamline adds a level of complexity and difficulty. Our primary goal when dealing with progressions is to start simple and work our way up to more difficult. It is better to review easy skills than to jump into difficult ones too early. When we talk about flow, we mean how does one activity or skill transition from one to another. Good flow is when your swim skills move from one to another with a logical connection. There should be a connection between your two skills. If we work on going underwater with a game, the next skill should incorporate "going underwater" in it somehow. We can play "Buckethead" and then follow that with supported front glides. Buckethead is a going underwater game and during front glides we want swimmers to put their whole face in the water. The two activities are directly connected. The following list is an example of bad lesson flow:
Butterfly kick
Going underwater to get rings with flutter kicks
Breaststroke kicks on the side of the pool
Streamlines with freestyle
Butterfly arms on the deck
You can see how there is not direct connection between any two swim skills. We encourage you to use the side of the pool or the deck to teach swim skills. Use a combination of in water

84

and on deck activities. But, do not chain together unrelated different activities. In the above list no skill is connected, and no skill is repeated for emphasis. Each item falls into its own separate skill progression. Create swim lesson plans where each skill follows a progression and each activity flows to the next with a specific same skill connection. You may do 4 different activities that all work on going underwater, or 3 different activities that are all about butterfly kick.

Progressions are logical sequential steps that connect two different things. Use progressions like stairs to take small steps towards a skill. If you want to teach a swimmer how to do freestyle break it into parts and go slow moving from the most basic fundamental skill and building on it. The first section of this book is intended to give you those progressive steps. If you have something new, start with the simplest explanation of that skill before asking participants to do it.

We do not want to tell a swimmer to "swim butterfly" unless they know all the pieces: streamline, fly kick, fly arms, fly breathing. We also want to make sure they have the endurance to do the activity well for whatever distance you ask. Shorter distances are better for beginners. They can put more mental effort into 2 or 3 strokes instead of the overwhelming stress of swimming a full length of a pool unsupported.

Small steps up
- Do activities that start off achievable then get slightly harder with each iteration.
- Put your face in the water, then float with support, then glide by yourself.

Have a goal
- What skill are you building to? What is at the top of the stairs?
- Start off easy, and get more difficult as you progress.

Interrupt flow
- Games and fun activities like challenges reset attention and can turn a wild class into a calm one.

Discussion Items:

What are the 3 general ideas to consider when you create a lesson plan?

Does age make a difference when you think about your swimmers?

Describe the difference between progression and flow.

How to handle going underwater

Give a choice, even if limited.

Earn your swimmer's trust.

Swimming's most fundamental skill is to "go underwater."

Swimming Ideas uses going underwater as the benchmark for our first level.

If you can easily and repeatedly go underwater on your own, then teaching all the rest of swimming becomes much easier.

You will notice from our level 1 activities that everything is designed to promote going underwater or accommodating non-underwater going persons.

Each activity should at some point have an opportunity to put your face in the water. The only exception to going underwater and swimming is backstroke.

It is the only stroke where the whole face does not submerge, but often we see beginners who don't like their face underwater also do not like putting their ears in the water on backstroke.

Every activity in level 1 should have some opportunity for the participant to go underwater on their own.

We recommend that you give every swimmer an option when beginning:

"Do you want to go underwater"

Or

"Put your face in the water" and if met with a "No." Adjust and say, "Put your chin in the water."

Then follow the underwater progression to incrementally move from not going underwater to full submersion.

We give swimmers a choice about going underwater because we want to earn their trust.

Earning trust is so important we devoted an entire section of this workbook to it.

When it comes to going underwater, we often see the most hesitation and fear.

When the swimmer trusts you, the instructor, they will be more likely to attempt things they are afraid of.

You can earn your swimmer's trust by asking if they want to go underwater for each activity, and here is the key part, by following through with their decision.

If the swimmer does not want to go underwater on a jump, a front glide, or a kick, modify the activity so they do not go underwater.

It is not giving in, and it seems like it might fly in the face of our ultimate goal: for them to go underwater.

Instead, it establishes a clear example that the swimmer can trust you.

When they trust you, they will begin to start listening to all of your commands and begin attempting things they might not have before.

You can earn trust multiple ways, and for going underwater, this is an excellent way to earn that swimmer's trust: give them a choice about going underwater.

Go slow
- Going underwater is a difficult and scary thing.
- Offer multiple times in different ways to go under.
- Give choices and adhere to the swimmer's choice.

Ask often
- "Do you want to go under?"
- Before doing a jump ask if the swimmer wants to go under. If they say no, listen. Ask frequently in every skill you do.

Entice with fun
- Build going underwater into every activity you do. Provide multiple opportunities to do it.

Discussion Items:

Why would we give beginners a choice in whether they go underwater or not? Why would we ask, "Do you want to go underwater?"

Come up with a specific example how you would persuade a beginner who says "No" to you when you ask them to put their face in the water during an assisted front float.

Why is "going underwater" the first skill we work on in swim lessons?

Incremental Underwater Progression

Follow the steps, going point by point.
Avoid skipping steps.
If met with a "no" go down a step.

Underwater Progression:

- Chest
- Shoulders
- Chin
- Lips
- Nose
- Eyes
- Whole Head

Before we complete the progression, we will add a few steps to help going underwater. When you are working with the youngest swimmers, you should start with pouring water over their head.

This has a different progression that is close to the full underwater progression. Start with pouring water on the shoulders. Then, move to pouring water on the back of the neck.

Next, pour water on the back of the head over the hair. Let the water drip down over the hair and fall down the back of the neck.

Our goal is to have the water over the head sensation exist but not coming down on the face yet.

After the participant is comfortable with water over the hair on the back of their head, we will slowly move the water forward on the top of the head. Start your pouring at the back of the head, and bring it forward to fall over the face.

For pouring water the progression is:

- Shoulder pour
- Back of the neck pour
- Back of the head, where water drains down the back of the head

Starting pour at the back of the head and bringing the water forward to the face.

You can use both progressions in a general way to get someone to go underwater. Start with a body part lower on the body and slowly work your way up.

If you are working with a swimmer that does not put their whole head underwater and you ask them to put their whole face in they will likely stare at you unmoving.

You will likely get push-back or a refusal from the participant. Instead, begin with a, "put your face in the water," and when met with a "no" or inaction, adjust your command to the most basic step of the progression they have not already done. If you are doing a supported front glide and you ask the participant to put their face in the water, and they say "no," change the command to "put your chin in the water." We move directly to chin because they already have their chest and shoulders in the water. Our goal is to have the participant willingly place a body part in the water with the support and encouragement of the instructor.

When we start with the most basic element, in this case the chin, we are more likely to get a favorable reaction. Our goal is to get the participant to go underwater, and beginning with the chin opens that door. Once the participant has easily put their chin in the water, we should challenge them to also put their lips in the water. We should move slowly through each step of the progression to give the participant a chance at easily moving from one stage to the next. If we jump ahead in the progression, we are more likely to be met with resistance and hesitation.

Pretend that we are doing a supported front glide with someone that does not go underwater completely on their own. They will put their arms out in front of themselves, will reach out to the instructor, but will not put their face in the water.

Their chest and shoulders are in the water as the instructor walks backwards supporting the participant at the surface. Here is a sample script:

"Put your hands on my shoulders and keep your arms straight." "Kick your feet the whole time. Well done! Okay, you are keeping your arms straight and kicking your feet, attempt to also put your face in the water." When met with resistance, "Then put your chin in the water like this." The instructor should do it too. "Excellent! Great job putting your chin in. Now let's blow bubbles with our lips in the water like this."

The instructor should give positive praise each time that the participant follows a command. When pushing hard, like asking for the full face to go under, adapt quickly and adjust your command to an achievable goal. In this case, switch from whole face to just the chin, and work your way up to lips, nose, eyes, and eventually whole face.

Key Take-aways:

Move slowly through each step of the underwater progression.

Avoid jumping over one of the steps. It is important to move through each one slowly. Attain comfort and ease with each stage.

Move to the next step when you are met with zero hesitation and when the participant will remain underwater for a prolonged period. For example, 5 seconds with lips held underwater easily.

Start easy.
- Begin with asking swimmers to put their chest in the water. Most will.
- Move up to the shoulders and progressively, one at a time ask for more.

Get harder
- Push against the swimmer's highest level of comfort. If they resist at putting their nose in. Ask twice for the nose in the water.
- Keep asking.

Praise each round!
- No matter what activity your swimmers do praise the effort. If they attempt, give them a high five!

Discussion Items:

Why would we begin by pouring water over the back of the head?

Is it okay to skip steps in the underwater progression?

When do you know your participant is ready for the next stage of the progression? Is it the same for everyone?

Addressing Fear

Remain calm, everything's going to be fine.

Swimming can be a scary thing. The water is different from the air, and adults act strangely around water. Sometimes the parents will hype up the importance of water safety so much that the participants in swim lessons are so terrified they immediately cry.

There are many different ways to address fear in a child, and we are going to look at a few of them in a swim lesson context. Before we look at how to address fear, we will identify some common reasons a child cries in swim lessons.

- They are away from their parents with strangers.
- The water is too cold and uncomfortable.
- The participant does not want to do it; not getting their way.
- The parent is frightened and the child notices it, and in turn is scared.
- The swimmer had a bad experience with swimming in the past.
- They are afraid of the swim instructor.

There are likely many more reasons why a child might be frightened and begin crying at swimming lessons. Our goal is to address that fear in a positive way that gets rid of the tears and screaming. We want to turn those tears into fun filled smiles where the participant is excited to be at swim lessons. Now that we have a general idea WHY a swimmer might cry or be afraid, we need to identify the different types of crying and fear.

Hesitation and refusal

This is the first warning sign of a frightened child at swim lessons. You may see this behavior before the swim lesson. The child might cling to the parent and avoid eye contact with the pool manager or swim instructor. They might hide physically behind the parent to protect themselves. Usually you see the lips turn into a frown and the eyes well up with tears. When pressed they will struggle, attempt to get their way, and often when forced to enter the pool with the instructor will cry with tears.

This might even manifest in the pool during a swim lesson. An otherwise happy participant might turn into the 'hesitation and refusal' swimmer when you require them to do something they absolutely do not want to. Sometimes if you say, "Okay, we're going to go underwater now," you might see this person go from smiles to wide-eyed fearful look.

They might attempt to turn away from you the instructor, or hide behind other participants. If you force them to take a turn they might begin crying to stop the activity from happening to them.

Panic and crying

If you pressure or force someone to participate that is displaying "hesitation and refusal," they might transition to full on panic mode. When this happens the child typically attempts to run from you, or baring that starts screaming aloud.

We should never get to the full panic and crying stage.

Our goal will be to adjust our behavior to accommodate before our participants get into panic and frightened hysterical crying. If for some reason you get to this stage here are some ways you can soothe the tears and reassure the parents.

Remain calm. We should remain calm and not react with additional yelling, fear or confusion ourselves. Remember, we are in control of the lesson and the authority figure in the water.

Act with confidence and gentle calm.

Avoid coddling. We do not want to go into hurt puppy mode and pick up with child and hug them telling them everything is okay. Instead, remain clam, offer support at a quiet volume, and provide comfort in your stability. We are not caving in to the child's demands, but we will listen to their concern and accommodate their expressed fears with modified activities.

Provide distraction.

When someone is in full on panic mode sometimes it is because we asked him or her to do something they are terrified of doing (like going underwater, or their parent not being visible).

We can distract them with a toy to play with, a group game, or an easily successful game. Place an item in the child's hands or redirect their motion to something they can easily do. This has 2 benefits: 1) they get in the habit of doing what you tell them, and 2) they focus on the activity and not what initially set off the meltdown.

Delay with a demonstration. Sometimes when we ask someone who is fearful already to do something they are terrified of first they panic and cry. Take another person in your class and do a modified version to demonstrate what the activity will look like.

Encourage your hesitating and fearful child to watch as you do a "no underwater jump" or "no underwater front float with support" before you give them their turn. When they see someone else do an activity, they will be more receptive to doing it themselves.

Turn to your deck manager, or call in parent reinforcements. Sometimes there is nothing we can do.

Do not sacrifice the rest of your class to accommodate the needs of one disruptive person. We attempt, distract, listen, and move on.

Call over your deck supervisor to help, or remove the child from the water and call over a parent.

When it is time to remove the crying child from the class

There are times when you will leave a kid who is crying in the class. Sometimes that child will be crying the whole time. That is okay if they still participate and respond to commands from the instructor. There are children that just need to sob to work out their emotions. Sometimes, that crying is so disruptive to the group and not productive for the crying person that we need to remove them from the lesson.

Generally, this should be the last resort after we have exhausted the above attempts to address panic and crying. Here are a few clear times when you should absolutely remove a child from the water and get them to the side with a manager or with their parent.

Child is crying so loudly and so intensely you cannot talk to them, they will not listen, and their shrieks drown out all other noise around them, destroying any opportunity for instruction in their immediate vicinity.

The child refuses to listen to the instructor for even the most basic of commands AND behaves in reckless and unsafe ways. There are times when a fearful child will refuse to participate, and sometimes that is fine. We offer repeatedly for them to do something, and move on. Let them sit there doing nothing while others have fun. It is time to remove the fearful child when they are attempting to crawl over the bench and run away, or when they ignore you and attempt to leave the group on their own. We need to provide a safe exit and it is better for us to make that choice than to allow the child to "escape" on its own.

Remove the child when they disrupt the class with physical lashing out; hitting, biting, clawing, or flailing their limbs. This can cause damage to you, others, or themselves and should not be tolerated.

There are other times to remove a fearful or crying child. Many of those times are specific to the child and the instance. These are some general archetypal examples to give you an understanding. Can you think of other examples of when we should remove a fearful child from a class?

Don't panic! They can smell your fear! How you react to a fear sets the tone. Be compassionate, gentle, caring.

Specific ways to address fear:

Reassurance.

I am here for you.
This is often the first tactic most swim instructors use to calm a frightened child. Often we reassure the swimmer by reminding them that we are there to help them and hold them when they cannot touch the bottom on their own. Remember, swimming and sinking can be very scary and we need to remember that. We need to build trust and we can do that by proving we are there to support the swimmer. Refer back to "earning trust through repeated honesty" to get more tactics on how to earn trust.

Acknowledge.

Tell the swimmer you understand their fear; give specific examples of how you will help that individual.

Do this without offering reasons for them to be afraid: "Are you scared of going underwater?"

Whenever possible, let the swimmer know you heard their fear and acknowledge it.

"I know you're a little afraid of this. We can do it together." Verbally take note of their fear or hesitation without giving a name to it, and then follow up with a reassurance.

"I know you are afraid, we will do this together and you do not have to go underwater."

Example.

Have someone else do the activity to demonstrate it.

This is straightforward. If you announce what the group is doing and you notice someone start displaying the typical fear signs (hiding, tearing up, crying, wide eyes) then start with someone who is not afraid and do a basic demonstration with them where you address the fear the child might have.

For example, if you are doing front glides and Johnny is afraid of putting his face in the water, take Sally, do a face out of the water front glide, and tell Johnny that he is going to do the exact same thing. **DO NOT demonstrate with someone more advanced that does go underwater and have him or her do so alone. You will only scare Johnny more.

Adaptation.

Changing activity to adjust to special singular needs. Continuing the front glide example, if Johnny does not like going underwater but Sally, and the rest of the group doesn't mind. Have everyone but Johnny do the underwater part and make specific language and instruction clear that Johnny does not HAVE to go underwater.

He may need to put his chin, lips, or nose in, but not his whole head. Here we are slightly adapting the expectation to accommodate the personal comfort level of the participant. Not everyone in a "level" is capable of doing everything the exact same. Make small adjustments to the same overall skill to accommodate each individual.

Steamroll.

Ignoring the stated fear and requiring participant to do action. If you know your class well, and if you know the participant well they may be using "fear" as a tactic to delay participation in an activity.

Not because they are afraid, but

92

for whatever reason, they don't want to do it. In this case, you ignore the protests and have the child participate. I cannot stress enough that this should only be used as a tactic to cure "fear" when you are certain that the child is not actually afraid and is instead doing a power play for attention or the upper hand with you, the instructor.

Sometimes you need to ignore the words and just do the activity. Again, use this ONLY when you are fully certain the "fear" you see expressed is a cover for some other thing.

Routine.

When you do things close to the same every time participants know what to expect and will not be surprised by scary new things.

One of the best reasons to follow the swim lesson plans we provide is this very reason: routine. When everyone teaches the same skills the same way with the same progression the swimmers know what to expect.

Knowing what comes next and what the framework is allows you to be more creative with how you accomplish your teaching goals.

The swim lesson plans we use set up the framework for what to teach.

This workbook shows you HOW to teach those skills (section 1) with specific activities and class setups. Be consistent across your classes and you'll see quicker results and less hesitant swimmers.
If you always go from bench to bench, how you do it can change, but the swimmer will move with confidence and familiarity because they've done it 100 times already. You can substitute different actions to get from bench to bench and you'll be met with zero or little hesitation and fear because they have already achieved success before.

Empathize

- How do you feel when confronted with fear?
- I'm terrified of flying, thinking about it gives me sweats. I avoid it. How can you address fear compassionately?

Be caring

- Compassion, gentle care, honesty, happiness, and hope will always win over gruff domineering behavior with children and going underwater.
- Approach fear with care.

Respect choices

- Parents will want you to "push" their kids because they want someone to be "tough on them."
- Avoid needlessly forcing a balking child to participate.
- Encourage, go slow, and welcome with fun.

Discussion Items:

What are at least 6 reasons a child might cry at swim lessons?

Should you provide suggestions to why a child might be scared? Example: "Are you crying because the water is cold?"
What should you do when a parent asks questions like this?

How can you create routine in your lessons to reduce fear in your swim lessons?
When should you remove a child physically from a class? (in a scared context, not misbehavior)

How can you keep yourself from panicking when a child starts crying?

Dunking versus Scooping

Do no dunk.

Give clear expectations.

Avoid forced submersions whenever possible.

At some point you're going to be forcing a child to go underwater. You may know this as the dreaded "dunking." We want you to provide the safest, and most effective way of dunking without causing the child or swimmer lasting emotional harm.

We reviewed how to earn the trust of your swimmer earlier.

You can do that by repeatedly being in the same place when they push off the wall, or bench.

You can be a consistent force of protection and help.

You can ask them to do small achievable goals to slowly build up their confidence and trust in you. You can also gradually introduce them to new things in a loving and safe environment.

The key to getting a child to go underwater and to keep them coming back to your program, and have a healthy positive relationship with swimming is to give them a safe, loving, and nurturing environment.

There are programs that throw kids in the water despite their screaming, crying, and thrashing.

DO NOT THROW A CHILD IN THE WATER.

Do not embrace the "sink or swim" mentality.

It will scar the child and create a negative association with the water.

The best way to get a child to go underwater is to repeatedly expose them to a pool that has a loving and nurturing environment. A positive experience will have better long term effects for the child, and the family.

Dunking, is the same thing as throwing a child in the water and forcing them to sink or swim. It is akin to activating their fight or flight response.

Vertical dunking. NOT RECOMMENDED.

Doing a vertical dunk like this will cause a "falling" sensation, and lead to hesitation, fear, and distrust.

Scooping

The recommended alternative to "dunking' is to scoop your swimmers. This is a gradual, incremental step by step process similar to everything else we do.

Remember the "underwater progression?"

Shoulders

Chin

Lips

Nose

Eyes

Whole head.

We will follow the same progression for Scooping. Begin at the lowest comfortable step on the progression and move no more than one step up at a time. Go from nose to eyes, not nose to whole head.

How to Scoop, and why it is different than dunking.

When you scoop, you're generally holding the child in a football catching position. Your hands are grasped around the child's torso, or you're supporting with your palms on their chest and ribs. They are laying flat, and will begin with their face about the water. Instead of dropping your hands and letting the child fall, we are going to hold them tight, and pull them through the water as we step backwards.

Scoop by taking a step backwards.

As you do, pull the child in a "U" shape with a gradual downward slope. Pull back, the deepest part of your "U" should be where the child's face goes to the progressive step; chin, nose, eyes, etc.

Start the scoop by stepping back, and putting just the shoulders in the water. Second scoop can be pulling the child down enough to get their chin wet.

Give excessive praise.

Over time, with gradual slow repetitive actions build up to getting the whole head underwater.

Moving water

- Most fear comes from water going up the nose or not breathing.
- Pulling keeps water from slamming up the nostrils.
- Scoop to remove pain.

Cue: 1, 2, 3.

- Give a mental preparation. 1, 2, 3, scoop.
- A verbal cue makes it easier for swimmer to get their breath and not be scared by a sudden submersion.

Smile. Give praise

- Regardless of response smile. Give excessive praise. Celebrate the attempt.

Discussion Items:

How do you feel about forcing a child to go underwater?

How can you prepare a swimmer for going underwater?

Should you include the parents in a discussion about doing a scoop with a child at swim lessons?

Scooping progression

Go slow.

Be gentle, encouraging, compassionate.

When you start taking your swimmers underwater, remember to use the same logical incremental progression process we use with everything else. Do the first easy step, then slowly one step at a time move on to the next step.

For scooping, for going underwater, we want to follow a similar progression to the Underwater Progression.

1) Shoulders
2) Chin
3) Lips
4) Nose
5) Eyes
6) Whole head

When your participant gets comfortable enough with one stage of the progression, move on to the next.

For example, if you have a swimmer that is comfortable putting their shoulders and chin in the water, after a clear explanation of what is going to happen, you would do the supported front glide hold, and on the count of three, step back and pull them underwater only going up to their chin.

Give praise to the swimmer for participating. Once they are comfortable with the chin in the water scoops and they do not hesitate or react poorly when you announce it as the next activity move on to the lips.

indicate that the next scoop will be with the lips underwater and show them how to close their lips. Demonstrate what it looks like for you to put your lips in.

You can do this with the swimmer next to you, or holding them in front with the football or palm up position hold.

Of most importance is to go slow!

Follow the gentle and comfortable progression where the child is relaxed and at ease with each step.

We want to avoid associating fear and anxiety about dunking and going underwater.

Remember to go slow!

The scooping progression is a gentle and slow process that should be taken with care and diligence.

Remember that we want to establish a healthy, safe, can caring environment for our youngest swimmers. We want them to be comfortable, relaxed, and happy.

The first stages of the scooping progression are more about establishing the "habit" and the expectation for the infant or young swimmer.

We are giving them a new stimuli and teaching them to expect a certain flow of actions. New, different, dropping, and water can be terrifying for infants and young swimmers.

Start with not going underwater at all, set up your cuing, aim the child's face at yours and pull them into a smiling embrace.

We want the child staring at the parent because most young swimmers do not have "object permanence." If the infant cannot see them that person does not exist.

Keep the parent in the infant's field of view to maintain a calm demeanor.

Count to three, "One, Two, Three," or whatever your consistent cue is, then pull the child into a hug, taking a step back to increase the traveled distance.

Smile, laugh, hug, and give praise.

Repeat.

Eventually the swimmer will be comfortable with the motion and the action and you can begin putting the chin in the water.

When they are bored and comfortable with the chin, do the lips, and so on.

Each step should be done with attention to the child's reaction. We want them to be at ease, relaxed, and happy.

Go slow, take your time and tell your parents in the classes that this is a slow process and not to rush through the progression.

You will have some parents in your infant classes that want to dunk their kids too quick. Do your best to calmly explain why it is important for them to go slow and be consistent.

Startling motions, loud noises, unexpected underwater, and aggressive dunking can lead to trauma, reluctance, and negative associations with water.

Our goal is to create long healthy relationships with swimming and that begins with a slow gradual process of going underwater.

We are in no rush to get infants to go underwater.

Rushing through dunking and scooping can teach infants and beginners to be afraid of the water. Avoid aggressive dunking or too fast scooping progressions by educating parents of the potential negatives.

Be consistent

- Repeat the same cuing words, "1, 2, 3." or "ready, go."
- Hold your hands the same way every time.
- Follow standard holds.

Take your time

- Start with the shoulders, then the chin.
- Move through the progression slowly until comfortable.
- Reign in wild parents.

Resist the urge

- Parents will want quick results.
- Fight the urge to listen.

Discussion Items:

Why is it better to go slow and be gentle with forcing kids to go underwater?

When is it appropriate to scoop/dunk a child?

How can we make something scary like going underwater less frightening?

Parent and Infant: How to hold

Keep the head above water, be gentle.

Horizontal floating, at surface best.

Football Hold

Key Points of Football Hold:

- Thumbs are on front of participant's chest
- Fingers are wrapped around sides touching back or shoulder blades
- Hold like the child is the football, and you are "catching" it.
- Easy to rotate participant forward on to their belly
- Easy to scoop
- Ideal for front glides.

Excellent for:

- Front Glides for beginners
- Keeping face to face connection (participant can see you)
- Blowing bubbles
- Putting chin, lips, nose, eyes in the water
- Scooping underwater

Not good for:

- Back floats
    - Feet point into chest if doing this hold
- Awkward to move in same direction
    - When held to the side

Reverse Football Hold

Use this hold to support swimmers who do not want to go underwater and who do not like to put their ears in the water. Place your shoulder under their head and maintain an instructor cheek to swimmer cheek connection. This will help keep the swimmer calm.

Key Points of Reverse Football Hold

- Instructor's thumbs should press into the shoulder blades, or back of swimmer.
- Wrap fingers around front of swimmer's chest.
- Instructor can easily rotate swimmer forward or back to control the horizontal orientation of the swimmer's body.
    - Goal is to get as close to the water and as flat on the surface as the swimmer is comfortable.
- Used primarily for assisted back floats and back glides when the swimmer does not like to get their ears underwater
- Useful when walking backwards, as the motion will lift the feet up to the surface.

Excellent for:

- Back floats
- Back glides
- Getting ears gently in the water
- Controlling body rotation and orientation to promote horizontal body position.

Not ideal for:

- Front floats where instructor is to the side
- Working on kicking as instructor's hands are occupied
    - Feet generally rise too high or low when body held like this.
- Swimmers that can relax and put their ears and whole head gently in the water. Different hold is a better choice.

Be gentle
- Move slow, like you're in a movie doing slowmow.
-
- Smile no matter what
-
- Laugh, be respectful, and hold with careful grip.

Ask for permission
- Before you reach or hold a child ask the parent if you can hold of work with their child.
-
- Parents know their kids. Some will freak out in a stranger's arms.

Aim at parent
- Always aim the infant's face at the parent when possible. A familiar face is calming.

Front and Back float palm up supports.
Like lifting a bowl up from the bottom, hold the child.

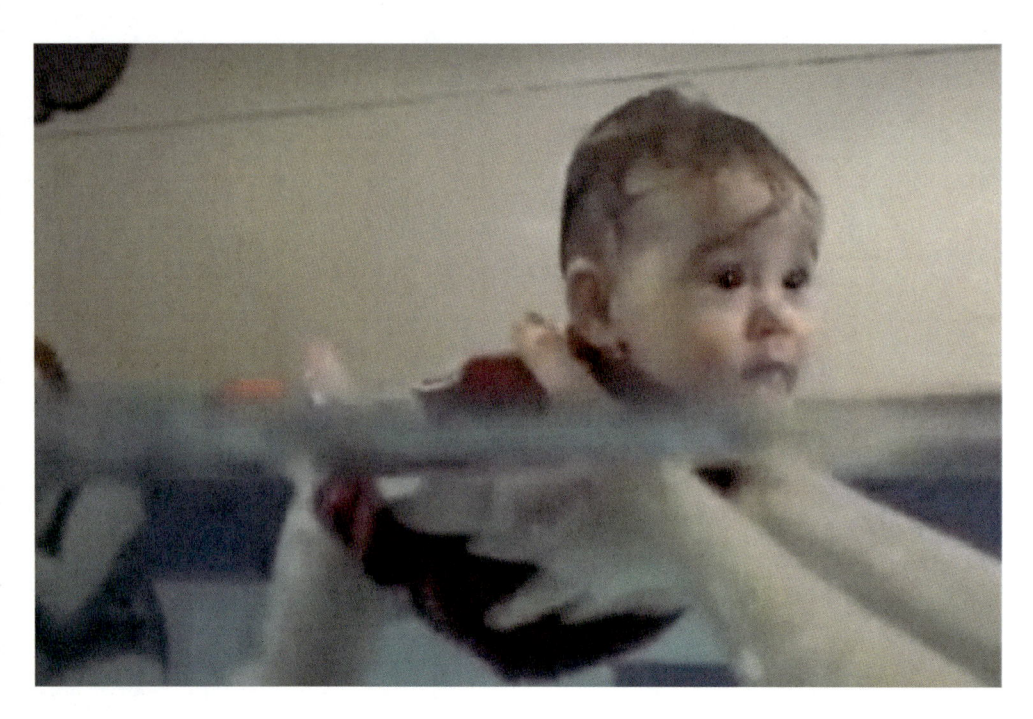

Front Float Palm Up support for smaller swimmers:

Here, we place our pinky fingers from each hand close together with our palms up.

The instructor lifts the child's chest on their open palms face up, and allows the child's weight to fall onto their hands.

You can easily control depth and encourage kicking using this hold.

It can be more effective for smaller and younger swimmers than the football position described before.

Key Points of Front Float Palm Up support:

Swimmer's chest rests in the upturned palms of the instructor (or parent).

Gently wrap fingers around participant's torso and shoulders to maintain balance and grip.

Let the weight of the swimmer dictate depth and gently support up with hands.

Walk backwards to simulate motion.

Excellent hold for drifting, scoops, and chin, lip, nose submersion.

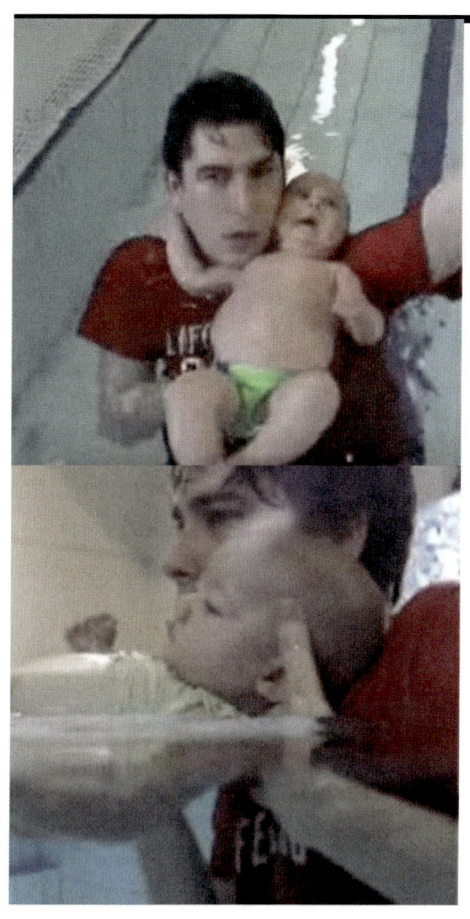

Head on shoulder supported hold

We rest the child's head on the shoulder of the instructor, or parent.

Aim for a cheek-to-cheek connection.

Maintain a physical connection with the cheek to make the swimmer feel more comfortable.

Lower your shoulders to be just under the water.

Let the swimmer's head rest solidly and firmly on your shoulder.

Use your hands to support the torso at the surface.

To transition to from a head on shoulder, move your hand under the child's head and support crown with your open palm.

Key points to "head on shoulder back float support"

- Let swimmer's head rest firmly on instructor's shoulder
- Instructor's cheek should be pressed against swimmer's cheek
- Use hands to support swimmer's body at the surface
    - Can use hands to "kick" the swimmers feet too
- Walk backwards slowly to give sensation of movement

Palms up.

- Let the child's weight rest in your upraised palms.
- Let the child float as much as possible, keeping the face above the water. Water line should be at shoulders and neck.

Level of comfort

- Avoid pushing too much, but hold the child at the surface of the water to their level of comfort.
- Beginners will be higher up and heavier.

Move!

- While holding walk backwards.
- Constant movement and motion makes the child's legs float near the surface and the flow of water helps keep their body straight and flat instead of solely relying on the instructor's hands.
- Move slow, sing, keep eye contact sand give toys to distract.

Worksheet 1 answers

1) What is the underwater progression?

Chest, shoulders, chin, lips, nose, eyes, whole head.

2) What does incremental progression mean?

Do things one after another without jumping out of sequence. Follow the steps, move slowly from step to step without skipping anything essential.

3) If we ask a swimmer, "Do you want to go underwater" and they say, "no," should you pull them underwater? Why?

No. We should not pull them under without adequate preparation or early advance warning. Surprise dunking can lead to trauma and we want a loving, caring, compassionate environment for swimmers to learn in.

4) What is the supported front glide script?

"Put your shoulders in the water", "Reach our arms out in front of you.", "Put your [chin, lips, nose, eyes, face] in the water.", "Push off with me."

5) When working with young swimmers in shallow water why is it important for the instructor to put their shoulders in the water too?

The swim instructor sets the tone and example for the rest of the class. If the instructor is gasping about how cold the water is and resisting going under than the swimmers won't either. It also makes it significantly more difficult to connect and earn trust. You must have shoulders in to do most of the supported glides and holds.

6) What are the benefits of demonstrating a swim skill first? Who can do the demonstrations?
Some swimmers learn better by watching someone else do a skill. We learn visually and seeing it can be more effective than words.

Anyone can demonstrate! Use lesson plans, skill sheets, or images on a TV or screen to help illustrate your skills!

7) Is it better to lead through fear or respect and trust?

TRUST! Fear leads to avoidance, reluctance, and hesitation. Earn trust and your swimmers will follow every word you say and perform well!

Worksheet 2 answers

1) Describe how a flutter kick begins and what moves.

This flutter kicks starts with the hips and rolls past the knees through the ankles with the feet being floppy. Each foot is like a individual fly kick.

2) What are the three key points to streamline? What is the Streamline Script?

1, Lock your thumb. 2. Squeeze your ears. 3. Look down. Same thing for both. Do it with everything.

3) Is it difficult for young children to do a perfect streamline? Why or why not?

Yes. Many will be off balance and struggle to swim or move with their arms reaching above their head. It takes a mix of flexibility and strength to do well and many younger swimmers may struggle significantly with it. Feel free to start with 11 for the 3-4 year olds.

4) What language would you use to describe or instruct someone who has never swam to do freestyle arms on deck?

Start in 11, push down in front of your body, at the swim suit end or beginning swing out to airplane, then return to position 11 above your head.

5) At first what will provide the most forward movement for beginners to freestyle? **Arm strokes** or **kicks**

The kicks! For many the idea, concept and feel of pushing the water to move forward is unknown. Most young swimmers will instinctively kick to provide propulsion.

6) What is soldier position?

Standing with spine straight, chin slightly tucked in, hands by the hips.

7) What is position 11?

Standing in soldier, but with your arms raised directly over your head above the shoulders. Arms parallel like an "11."

8) For beginners should you worry about how the elbow bends or if the hands are cupping or scooping the water?

No. Worry more about the large circular motions of the arms. The fine motor motions like hands scooping do not matter for beginners. Avoid the "pretty" swimming.

Worksheet 3 answers

1) What is position 11? Describe in detail, or draw a picture:

Position 11 is standing with body straight, chin and head stacked above the spine, arms raised above the shoulders with elbows straight.

2) What is the script you'd use to introduce breaststroke arms to a beginner?

"11, Eat and breathe, 11."

3) TRUE or FALSE : SL + Flex is an activity where there is no kick and the swimmer glides off the wall with toes turned apart and raised.

False. Streamline with "flex" position is a push off the wall where the toes flair out. Described above is "lift and flex."

4) How will a "vampire neck" hurt a swimmer's backstroke?

Lifting the chin up will expose the neck and promote a banana or rainbow shape to the body while the swimmer moves. It will push more water and make the stroke wobbly and difficult.

5) "Thumb, Hi, Pinky, Push" describes what swim motion?

Backstroke arms. Thumb comes out of the water. Wave hello to the people watching with a twist at the apex, and enter the water with your pinky.

6) Should the chin be slightly tucked in when swimming backstroke?

YES! A slightly tucked chin keeps the body flat when swimming on the back. Too much tuck is not good, so it should be very slight.

Worksheet 4 answers

1) What aquatic animal can we talk about to describe butterfly kick?

Dolphin! Flowing undulating dolphin kicks.

2) What is "undulation?" Describe in detail:

Undulation is where the body moves like doing the "wave." The chest pushes forward, then the belly, rolling down like a wave through the thighs, knees, and feet. The body continues to "undulate" in a waving motion where some parts are up and others down.

3) What are two things you can tell a swimmer to do to make a front flip easier?

Tuck your chin, and lift your butt. If you do that your feet will flop right over your head.

4) When swimming fly should the hips or butt rise above the surface with the kick when the arms are in position 11?

YES! When the arms sweep up from airplane position the hips should start rising to keep the kick and body undulation going. When the hips are up the arms are up.

6) TRUE or FALSE   When doing a flip turn you should push off on your back and rotate to your belly during the streamline while you are *not* touching the wall.

TRUE! Rotate after you've pushed off on your back.

7) Open turns are for what two strokes? What is the first step?

Breaststroke and Butterfly. The first step is to touch the wall with two hands, then get on your side throwing your elbow backwards.

Thank you! Good luck!

I appreciate you using this workbook to be a better swim instructor. My hope is that you've learned the basic swim skills that take you from a novice to a master swimmer. I also hope you found this guide to be an easy to read and follow blueprint for your future success. I will leave you with three quotes I have on my wall that help motivate me to improve.

"There are no limitations to the mind except those we acknowledge."

"Those who are afraid of new ideas are doomed before they start."

Napoleon Hill

"We are what we think. All that we are arises with our thoughts. With our thoughts, we make the world."

Prince Gautama Siddharta

Who am I and More information:

Jeffrey Napolski started teaching swim lessons when he was 16 at the local outdoor pool. He lifeguarded and taught swim lessons there for the next 7 summers. Jeff's competitive swimming was in high school as a junior and senior on the JV team. His best stroke and fastest time were a 100 Back at 1:00:06.

Jeff is a master swim game creator, and claims to have invented "Buckethead the best game ever." He has been teaching and running swim programs for 20 years, and now works for a USA Swimming club team with Level 4 Club Development.

He coaches Developmental swimmers and teaches lessons every week.

In the summers when he is not at a swim meet he vacations with his family in Door County Wisconsin. His favorite fitness activities right now are running, yoga, and biking.

Contact him now: jeff@swimmingideas.com

Twitter: @swimmingideas

See more guides, games, and lesson plans at www.swimminglessonsideas.com